MOVIE ★ ICONS

TAYLOR

EDITOR
PAUL DUNCAN

TEXT
JAMES URSINI

PHOTOS
THE KOBAL COLLECTION

TASCHEN

HONG KONG KÖLN LONDON LOS ANGELES MADRID PARIS TOKYO

CONTENTS

1

ELIZABETH TAYLOR: ETERNAL ROMANTIC

BY JAMES URSINI

ELIZABETH TAYLOR: DIE EWIGE ROMANTIKERIN

ELIZABETH TAYLOR: L'ÉTERNELLE ROMANTIQUE

ELIZABETH TAYLOR: ETERNAL ROMANTIC

by James Ursini

Elizabeth Taylor was a diva when that word still had meaning, before it was applied to every female celebrity with the slightest bit of attitude and style. Taylor was also one of the first actors to be elevated to celebrity status by the media for the dramatic conflicts of her personal life as much as for any thespian achievements on the screen. In the 1950s, when studios controlled what the media said about their valuable properties, Taylor's expansive personality and rollercoaster personal life were far too extravagant and exciting to be contained by Hollywood spin doctors.

But Taylor was not always a diva. She began her career as a child actress in the 1940s very much under the thumb of her pushy mother Sara. Schooled on the lot in the "little red schoolhouse" along with Louis B. Mayer's other stable of child actors, including lifelong friend Roddy McDowall, Taylor had a restricted and managed life. Once she became a verified star in *National Velvet* (1944), the supervision became even more oppressive. However, when she passed through puberty and developed very early the voluptuous figure and dark, exotic features she later became famous for (writer James Agee described her as 'rapturously beautiful'), Taylor also found her own inner strength, as well as an indomitable will that not even a studio as powerful as MGM could contain. Gradually freeing herself from the yoke of both her overbearing mother and her MGM contract, Taylor rebelled on all levels — personally, sexually, and creatively.

As Taylor's confidence blossomed, so did the quality of her acting. Comfortable now with her sexuality, which would always be a driving force in her numerous marriages and affairs as well as her best performances, she expressed a luminosity (centered often in her brilliant eyes) coupled with a smoldering sensuality and a petulant "little girl" quality in landmark roles in George Stevens' *A Place in the Sun* (1951) and *Giant* (1956) as well as in Edward Dmytryk's *Raintree County* (1957).

PORTRAIT (1954)

"If not to make the world better, what is money for?"
Elizabeth Taylor

The diva persona developed in those films bled over into her personal life, to the shock and delight of the public. Her attraction to husbands like hotel millionaire Nicholas Hilton and show-business magnate Mike Todd rested to a large degree on their ability to spoil her, while her attraction to bisexual friends like Montgomery Clift and James Dean and husbands Michael Wilding and Eddie Fisher fulfilled the dominant 'mothering gene' in her personality. Taylor's willingness to defy conventions, particularly of Hollywood and the 1950s, led her into battle after battle with the press. Her multiple love affairs and marriages made her more famous, or possibly infamous, than any film she made. As Taylor's controversial persona reached superstar status, she also began to gravitate towards more daring roles. In 1958 she played the sex-starved Maggie in Tennessee Williams' *Cat on a Hot Tin Roof*; in 1960 a prostitute in *BUtterfield 8* (for which she won her first Academy Award); and in 1961 she began work on the epic that would change her life as well as fix her image in the public mind forever — *Cleopatra*.

Taylor was born to play Cleopatra. She shared many characteristics with the Egyptian queen of history and legend. She loved wealth and power; she was sexually charged; and she was a romantic. And even though the film took years to make back its astronomical cost (estimated at $300 million if shot today) and met with some disastrous and patently vindictive reviews, to her loyal public Taylor *was* Cleopatra.

Taylor's romantic and professional relationship with actor Richard Burton also began with this movie and extended for over a decade. In the films she made with her new husband (*The Sandpiper*, 1965, *Who's Afraid of Virginia Woolf?*, 1966, *The Taming of the Shrew*, 1967, etc.), Taylor pushed her diva persona into the realms of the virago, giving both the negative and positive qualities of her personality free rein in the roles.

After her final break-up with Burton (there were many in their tempestuous, alcohol-driven relationship), Taylor married John Warner and helped him to become a Republican senator. Later, as many of her gay friends — including Rock Hudson — contracted the AIDS virus, she worked tirelessly for AIDS research funding. To her public Taylor has retained her iconic status, maintaining a hold on their admiration not only through her imperial beauty and her willingness to defy mores, but also through her unflagging romanticism.

ENDPAPERS/VOR- UND NACHSATZBLÄTTER/
PAGES DE GARDE
POSTER FOR 'DOCTOR FAUSTUS' (1967)

PAGES 2/3
STILL FROM 'THE TAMING OF THE SHREW' (1967)

PAGE 4
ON THE SET OF 'CLEOPATRA' (1963)

PAGES 6/7
ON THE SET OF 'CLEOPATRA' (1963)

PAGE 8
PORTRAIT

OPPOSITE /RECHTS /CI-CONTRE
PORTRAIT (1948)

ELIZABETH TAYLOR: DIE EWIGE ROMANTIKERIN

von James Ursini

Elizabeth Taylor war eine Diva, als das Wort noch eine Bedeutung hatte – bevor jede weibliche Berühmtheit so genannt wurde, die auch nur halbwegs einen Anflug von Haltung und Stil besaß. Taylor war auch eine der ersten Schauspielerinnen, die ihre Bekanntheit in den Medien genauso sehr den dramatischen Konflikten ihres Privatlebens verdankte wie ihrer schauspielerischen Leistung auf der Leinwand. In den fünfziger Jahren des vergangenen Jahrhunderts, als die Studios noch kontrollierten, was die Medien über ihren wertvollen „Besitz" (die Stars) berichteten, waren Taylors überschwängliche Persönlichkeit und die Achterbahnfahrten ihres Privatlebens viel zu aufregend und extravagant, um von den PR-Abteilungen in Hollywood gebändigt und in die erwünschten Bahnen gelenkt zu werden.

Aber Taylor ist nicht immer eine Diva gewesen. Sie begann ihre Karriere in den vierziger Jahren als Kinderstar, der sehr stark unter der Fuchtel seiner ehrgeizigen Mutter Sara stand. Sie drückte die Schulbank im „kleinen roten Schulhaus" von MGM, zusammen mit den anderen Kinderstars aus Louis B. Mayers Stall, darunter auch Roddy McDowall, mit dem sie zeit seines Lebens befreundet blieb. Ihr Leben wurde von Anfang an reguliert und von anderen bestimmt. Nachdem sie mit *Kleines Mädchen, großes Herz* (1944) zum echten Star aufstieg, wurde die Überwachung noch erdrückender. Als sie jedoch in die Pubertät kam und schon sehr früh die üppigen Formen und dunklen, exotischen Züge entwickelte, für die sie später berühmt wurde (der Schriftsteller James Agee beschrieb sie als „hinreißend schön"), fand Taylor auch ihre eigene innere Kraft und einen unbezwingbaren Willen, den nicht einmal ein so mächtiges Studio wie MGM zu bändigen vermochte. Nach und nach befreite sie sich aus dem Joch ihrer dominierenden Mutter und ihres MGM-Vertrags und rebellierte auf allen Ebenen – persönlich, sexuell und kreativ.

Als Taylors Selbstvertrauen aufblühte, reiften auch ihre schauspielerischen Qualitäten. Sie fühlte sich wohl mit ihrer Sexualität, die stets eine treibende Kraft in ihren zahlreichen Ehen und besten Darstellungen sein sollte. In den Rollen, die zu den Meilensteinen ihrer Karriere gehören,

PORTRAIT (1949)

„Wozu ist Geld gut, wenn nicht, um die Welt zu verbessern?"
Elizabeth Taylor

strahlte sie ein Leuchten aus, (in dessen Mittelpunkt oft ihre funkelnden Augen standen), gekoppelt mit einer glühenden Sinnlichkeit und einer launischen Mädchenhaftigkeit – wie etwa in *Eine amerikanische Tragödie* (1951) und *Giganten* (1956) von George Stevens oder *Das Land des Regenbaums* (1957) von Edward Dmytryk.

Die Rolle der Diva, die sie in diesen Filmen entwickelte, schwappte in ihr Privatleben über, zum Entzücken und Entsetzen der Öffentlichkeit. Zu Ehemännern wie dem Hotelmillionär Nicholas Hilton und dem Showgeschäftsmagnaten Mike Todd fühlte sie sich vor allem hingezogen, weil diese sie nach Strich und Faden verwöhnen konnten, während sie bei bisexuellen Freunden, wie Montgomery Clift und James Dean und ihren Ehemännern Michael Wilding und Eddie Fisher die mütterliche Seite ihres Charakters zum Ausdruck bringen konnte. Taylors Bereitwilligkeit, sich über Konventionen hinwegzusetzen – insbesondere die Hollywoods und die der fünfziger Jahre, führte zu immer neuen Auseinandersetzungen mit der Presse. Ihre zahlreichen Liebesaffären und Ehen machten sie berühmter – oder möglicherweise auch berüchtigter – als ihre Filme. Als Taylors umstrittene Persönlichkeit den Status eines Superstars erreicht hatte, traute sie sich an gewagtere Rollen heran. So spielte sie 1958 die sexhungrige Maggie in *Die Katze auf dem heißen Blechdach* nach dem Stück von Tennessee Williams, 1960 eine Prostituierte in *Telefon Butterfield 8* (für die sie ihren ersten Academy Award erhielt) und begann 1961 mit der Arbeit an einem Epos, das nicht nur ihr Leben verändern, sondern auch für alle Zeiten ihr Image in der Öffentlichkeit festigen sollte – *Cleopatra*.

Taylor war für die Rolle der Kleopatra wie geschaffen. Sie hatte vieles mit der historischen und legendären ägyptischen Königin gemeinsam. Sie liebte Wohlstand und Macht, war ausgesprochen sexuell und romantisch. Und obwohl es Jahre dauerte, bis der Film seine astronomischen Kosten (bei heutigen Verhältnissen würde er schätzungsweise 200 Millionen Euro kosten) eingespielt hatte, und die Kritiken teilweise vernichtend bis ausgesprochen bösartig waren, *war Taylor für ihr treues Publikum Kleopatra.*

Taylors private und berufliche Beziehung zu ihrem Kollegen Richard Burton begann ebenfalls mit diesem Film und zog sich über ein ganzes Jahrzehnt hin. In den Filmen, die sie mit ihrem neuen Ehemann drehte ... *die alles begehren* (1965), *Wer hat Angst vor Virginia Woolf?* (1966), *Der Widerspenstigen Zähmung* (1967) usw., erweiterte Taylor ihre Divenrolle in den Bereich der Xanthippe und ließ sowohl den negativen als auch den positiven Eigenschaften ihrer Persönlichkeit in diesen Rollen freien Lauf.

Nach ihrer endgültigen Trennung von Burton (es gab derer viele in ihrer stürmischen, vom Alkohol getriebenen Beziehung) heiratete Taylor John Warner und verhalf dem Republikaner zu einem Sitz im US-Senat. Später, als sich viele ihrer homosexuellen Freunde – darunter auch Rock Hudson – mit dem HI-Virus infiziert hatten, engagierte sie sich unermüdlich für die Subventionierung der AIDS-Forschung. Für ihre Fans ist Taylor nach wie vor eine Ikone, die sich ihrer Bewunderung gewiss sein kann – nicht nur aufgrund ihrer imperialen Schönheit und ihrer Bereitschaft, sich über Gepflogenheiten hinwegzusetzen, sondern auch aufgrund ihrer ungetrübten romantischen Ader.

PORTRAIT (1950)

ELIZABETH TAYLOR: L'ÉTERNELLE ROMANTIQUE

James Ursini

Elizabeth Taylor a été une diva à l'époque où ce mot avait encore un sens, avant qu'il ne soit systématiquement appliqué à toute célébrité féminine possédant un tant soit peu de personnalité et d'élégance. Liz Taylor a également été l'une des premières à être élevées au rang de célébrité par les médias en raison des drames qui agitaient sa vie privée autant que pour ses talents d'actrice. Dans les années 1950, époque où les studios contrôlent les informations qui circulent sur leurs précieuses vedettes, sa personnalité expansive et sa vie mouvementée sont bien trop extravagantes pour demeurer sous la coupe des spécialistes en communication d'Hollywood.

Mais Liz Taylor n'a pas toujours été une diva. Lorsqu'elle entame sa carrière à l'âge de dix ans, au début des années 1940, elle se trouve sous l'emprise d'une mère dévorée d'ambition. Scolarisée avec les autres jeunes acteurs (dont son ami de toujours, Roddy McDowall) dans les locaux mêmes de la Metro-Goldwyn-Mayer, elle mène une existence stricte et régentée. Lorsqu'elle devient une vedette dans *Le Grand National* (1944), l'étau se resserre encore. Cependant, lorsque la puberté la dote de la voluptueuse silhouette et de la beauté latine qui feront sa renommée, elle découvre en elle une force intérieure et une volonté indomptable que même un studio aussi puissant que la MGM ne parviendra pas à maîtriser. Se libérant peu à peu du joug de sa mère dominatrice et de son contrat avec la MGM, Liz Taylor se rebellera tant sur le plan personnel que sexuel et artistique.

À mesure que la jeune femme prend confiance en elle, son talent d'actrice s'épanouit. Assumant désormais l'érotisme qui sera toujours le moteur de ses nombreuses aventures sentimentales et de ses meilleures interprétations, elle mêle à la luminosité de son regard étincelant une sensualité torride et une irascibilité enfantine qui marqueront des films tels que *Une place au soleil* (1951) et *Géant* (1956) de George Stevens ou *L'Arbre de vie* (1957) d'Edward Dmytryk.

« À quoi sert l'argent, si ce n'est à rendre le monde meilleur ? »
Elizabeth Taylor

PORTRAIT

Le personnage de diva qui voit le jour dans ces œuvres a tôt fait de déteindre sur sa vie privée, attisant la curiosité et la réprobation du public. Son attirance pour des hommes richissimes tels que l'héritier des hôtels Hilton et le producteur Mike Todd découle en grande partie de leur capacité à assouvir ses moindres désirs, tandis que son amitié pour des bisexuels comme Montgomery Clift et James Dean et son mariage avec Michael Wilding ou Eddie Fisher reposent sur son instinct maternel et dominateur. Sa volonté de défier les conventions, en particulier celles d'Hollywood et des années 1950, lui fait mener d'incessantes batailles contre la presse. Ses diverses aventures et ses nombreux mariages la rendent plus (tristement) célèbre qu'aucun de ses films. Tandis que son personnage controversé accède au statut de star, l'actrice s'oriente vers des rôles plus audacieux. En 1958, elle incarne une épouse assoiffée de sexe dans *La Chatte sur un toit brûlant* de Tennessee Williams ; en 1960, elle campe une prostituée dans *Vénus au vison* (qui lui vaut son premier oscar) ; et en 1961, elle entame le tournage de l'épopée qui va bouleverser sa vie et graver à jamais son image dans l'esprit du public : *Cléopâtre*.

Elizabeth Taylor est née pour jouer Cléopâtre. Elle possède de nombreux points communs avec le personnage historique et légendaire de la reine d'Égypte. Comme elle, l'actrice aime la fortune et le pouvoir et abrite sous des dehors érotiques des sentiments romantiques. Et bien que le film ait mis des années à rentabiliser son coût astronomique (estimé à 300 millions de dollars actuels) et ait essuyé des critiques aussi désastreuses que vindicatives, Elizabeth Taylor est et restera Cléopâtre aux yeux de son fidèle public.

C'est également avec ce film que débute la relation professionnelle et sentimentale de Liz Taylor avec l'acteur Richard Burton, qui durera plus de dix ans. Dans les films qu'elle tourne avec lui – *Le Chevalier des sables* (1965), *Qui a peur de Virginia Woolf ?* (1966), *La Mégère apprivoisée* (1967), etc. –, elle donne à son personnage de diva des allures de furie, laissant libre cours aux aspects les plus négatifs et les plus positifs de sa personnalité.

Après sa dernière rupture avec Burton (il y en eut beaucoup dans leur relation orageuse placée sous l'emprise de l'alcool), Liz Taylor épouse le politicien républicain John Warner, qu'elle aide à devenir sénateur. Par la suite, voyant nombre de ses amis homosexuels – y compris Rock Hudson – contracter le SIDA, elle milite inlassablement pour le financement de la recherche contre le virus. Aux yeux de son public, Elizabeth Taylor a conservé son statut de légende, suscitant l'admiration non seulement par sa beauté impériale et ses nombreux défis aux bonnes mœurs, mais également par son inébranlable romantisme.

OPPOSITE/RECHTS/CI-CONTRE
PORTRAIT

PAGE 22
PORTRAIT

2

VISUAL FILMOGRAPHY

FILMOGRAFIE IN BILDERN

FILMOGRAPHIE EN IMAGES

PORTRAIT (1935)
Elizabeth with her mother, Sara, and brother Howard.
Elizabeth: "My mother was my best girlfriend, my guide,
my mentor, my constant companion." / Elizabeth mit
ihrer Mutter Sara und ihrem Bruder Howard.
Elizabeth: „Meine Mutter war meine beste Freundin,
meine Führerin, meine Mentorin, meine ständige
Begleiterin." / Elizabeth avec sa mère Sara et son frère
Howard. Elizabeth: « Ma mère était ma meilleure amie,
mon guide, mon mentor, ma compagne de tous les
instants. »

"I never wanted a career — it was forced on me."
Elizabeth Taylor

*„Ich wollte nie eine Karriere — man hat sie mir
aufgezwungen."*
Elizabeth Taylor

*« Je n'ai jamais voulu faire carrière ; on me l'a
imposé. »*
Elizabeth Taylor

PORTRAIT FOR 'THERE'S ONE BORN EVERY MINUTE' (1942)
Originally titled 'Man or Mouse,' this is Elizabeth's first film. The boy on the receiving end is 'Our Gang' star Carl "Alfalfa" Switzer. / Dieser Film, der ursprünglich den Titel *Man or Mouse* tragen sollte, war Elizabeths Erstling. Der Junge, dem sie hier die Ohren langzieht, ist Carl "Alfalfa" Switzer, der durch die Kurzfilmreihe *Die kleinen Strolche* berühmt wurde. / Dans son premier film, à l'origine intitulé *Man or Mouse*, Elizabeth s'en prend à Carl Switzer, alias Alfalfa, héros de la série *Les Petites Canailles*.

STILL FROM 'LASSIE COME HOME' (1943)
Elizabeth charms the first in a long line of older men
(Nigel Bruce), on and off screen. / Elizabeth lässt ihren
Charme beim ersten (Nigel Bruce) in einer langen Reihe
älterer Männer — auf der Leinwand wie hinter den
Kulissen — spielen. / Nigel Bruce, le premier d'une
longue lignée d'hommes mûrs charmés par l'actrice,
à la ville comme à l'écran.

"Constantly faced with adult situations and
denied the companionship of my peers, I stopped
being a child the minute I started working in
pictures."
Elizabeth Taylor

„Da ich ständig mit Erwachsenensituationen
konfrontiert war und mir die Gesellschaft
Gleichaltriger versagt war, hörte ich in dem
Augenblick auf, Kind zu sein, als ich anfing, beim
Film zu arbeiten."
Elizabeth Taylor

MGM'S SCHOOLHOUSE (1945)
A diligent Elizabeth at work in MGM's version of home schooling, the "little red schoolhouse." In fact, she was so shy she hid under the desk. / Eine fleißige Elizabeth bei der Arbeit in der MGM-Version des Schulunterrichts außerhalb des Systems: im „kleinen roten Schulhaus". Liz war damals so schüchtern, dass sie sich oft unter dem Tisch versteckte. / Elizabeth, que l'on voit étudier sagement dans la «petite école rouge» réservée aux jeunes acteurs de la MGM, était en réalité si timide qu'elle se cachait souvent sous son pupitre.

« Constamment confrontée à des situations d'adultes et privée de la compagnie de mes semblables, j'ai cessé d'être une enfant dès l'instant où j'ai commencé à faire des films. »
Elizabeth Taylor

"It's wrong to hate people."
Helen Burns, 'Jane Eyre' (1944)

„Es ist nicht recht, Leute zu hassen."
Helen Burns, *Die Waise von Lowood* (1944)

« C'est mal de détester les gens.»
Helen Burns, *Jane Eyre* (1944)

STILL FROM 'JANE EYRE' (1944)
A dark beauty already, Elizabeth is loaned out to
Twentieth Century Fox to play pious Helen Burns,
friend of the young Jane Eyre (Peggy Ann Garner). /
Schon damals war Elizabeth eine dunkelhaarige
Schönheit, die an Twentieth Century Fox ausgeliehen
wurde, um die fromme Helen Burns zu spielen, eine
Freundin der jungen Jane Eyre (Peggy Ann Garner). /
Déjà remarquée pour sa beauté latine, la jeune actrice
est prêtée à la Twentieth Century Fox pour interpréter
la pieuse Helen Burns, amie de Jane Eyre (Peggy Ann
Garner).

**STILL FROM 'THE WHITE CLIFFS OF DOVER'
(1944)**
Uncredited once again, Elizabeth plays Betsy Kenney
at the age of ten. / Wieder einmal ohne Nennung im
Vor- oder Abspann spielt die Elizabeth die Rolle der
zehnjährigen Betsy Kenney. / Elizabeth, qui ne figure
pas au générique, incarne Betsy Kenney à l'âge de dix
ans.

"My initial impression of her? She was Little Miss
Gorgeous."
Roddy McDowall

„Mein erster Eindruck von ihr? Sie war das kleine
Fräulein Wunderschön."
Roddy McDowall

« Ma première impression ? C'était une vraie petite
merveille. »
Roddy McDowall

**STILL FROM 'THE WHITE CLIFFS OF DOVER'
(1944)**
Elizabeth with one of her lifelong friends, Roddy
McDowall, another product of the Hollywood child star
system. / Elizabeth mit einem Freund fürs Leben,
Roddy McDowall, einem weiteren Produkt des Kinder-
starsystems von Hollywood. / En compagnie d'un de ses
amis de toujours, Roddy McDowall, autre enfant star
produit par l'industrie hollywoodienne.

STILL FROM 'NATIONAL VELVET' (1944)
Elizabeth's breakthrough film. After this performance
she became a star. / Der Film, der Elizabeth den
Durchbruch brachte. Nach diesem Auftritt war sie ein
Star. / Le film qui la révélera au public et fera d'elle une
vedette.

STILL FROM 'NATIONAL VELVET' (1944)
Velvet Brown wins a horse in a lottery, nurses it through
illness, and rides it to victory in the Grand National.
Elizabeth: "Some of my best leading men have been
dogs and horses." / Velvet Brown gewinnt ein Pferd in
der Lotterie, pflegt es, als es krank wird, und reitet es
beim Grand National zum Sieg. Elizabeth: „Einige
meiner besten Filmpartner waren Hunde und Pferde." /
Velvet Brown, qui gagne un cheval à la loterie, le soigne
pendant sa maladie et remporte avec lui le Grand
National. Elizabeth Taylor : « Certains de mes meilleurs
partenaires ont été des chiens et des chevaux. »

STILL FROM 'NATIONAL VELVET' (1944)
Although she could already ride, Elizabeth took rigorous riding lessons so that she could race on screen and get the part. During one lesson she suffered a fall, an injury which would cause her physical problems her entire life. / Obwohl sie bereits reiten konnte, nahm Elizabeth Reitunterricht für die Rennszenen, damit sie die Rolle bekam. In einer der Reitstunden fiel sie vom Pferd und zog sich eine Verletzung zu, unter der sie ihr ganzes Leben lang leiden würde. / Bien qu'elle sache déjà monter, Elizabeth suit un entraînement rigoureux pour décrocher le rôle. Lors d'une chute, elle subit une blessure dont elle gardera toute sa vie les séquelles.

STILL FROM 'NATIONAL VELVET' (1944)
Although this was considered by MGM to be a Mickey Rooney film, Elizabeth stole the show. / Wenn auch MGM den Film als Mickey-Rooney-Film betrachtete, stahl ihm Elizabeth die Show. / Bien que Mickey Rooney soit considéré par la MGM comme le héros du film, Elizabeth lui vole la vedette.

ON THE SET OF 'NATIONAL VELVET' (1944)
Cinematographer Leonard Smith congratulates Elizabeth. After the shoot, animal-lover Elizabeth was given the horse as a present. / Leonard Smith gratuliert Elizabeth. Nach den Dreharbeiten schenkte man der Tierfreundin Elizabeth das Pferd. / Leonard Smith congratule la jeune actrice amie des animaux, qui recevra sa monture en cadeau à l'issue du tournage.

ADVERTISING ARTWORK FOR 'NATIONAL VELVET' (1944)
Critic James Agee waxed poetic in his review and called her 'rapturously beautiful.' / James Agee ließ sich in seiner Filmkritik zu poetischer Schwärmerei verleiten und nannte Liz „hinreißend schön". / La jeune révélation suscite des élans lyriques chez le critique James Agee, qui salue sa « beauté envoûtante ».

M·G·M *presents*

LASSIE
IN A **NEW** ADVENTURE

COURAGE of LASSIE

ELIZABETH TAYLOR ★ **FRANK MORGAN** ★ **TOM DRAKE**

ORIGINAL SCREEN PLAY BY LIONEL HOUSER

Directed by FRED M. WILCOX *Produced by* ROBERT SISK

in Technicolor

A METRO-GOLDWYN-MAYER PICTURE

POSTER FOR 'COURAGE OF LASSIE' (1946)
Elizabeth and her mother rehearsed intensely, so that
during shooting Sara coached her daughter's
performance using hand signals. / Elizabeth und ihre
Mutter probten intensiv, sodass Sara ihrer Tochter
während der Dreharbeiten mit Handzeichen
Anweisungen geben konnte. / Elizabeth répète
assidûment avec sa mère Sara, qui la guide durant le
tournage à l'aide de signes des mains.

PORTRAIT FOR 'LIFE WITH FATHER' (1947)
MGM loaned Elizabeth out to Warner Bros. who paid
MGM more than five times her salary. / MGM liehen
Elizabeth an Warner Bros. aus, die ihnen das Fünffache
ihrer Gage zahlten. / MGM prête sa protégée à la
Warner et reçoit en contrepartie cinq fois le salaire
initial de l'actrice.

STILL FROM 'CYNTHIA' (1947)
With Mary Astor, a teenage Elizabeth begins to show
the voluptuous sensuality which will garner her the
adulation of both critics and fans all her life. / Neben
Mary Astor begann Elizabeth schon als Teenager, ihre
Sinnlichkeit zur Schau zu stellen, die ihr das ganze
Leben lang die Schwärmereien von Kritikern und Fans
sicherte. / Aux côtés de Mary Astor, l'adolescente laisse
poindre la voluptueuse sensualité qui lui vaudra toute sa
vie l'adulation de la critique et de ses fans.

"I have a woman's body and a child's emotions."
Elizabeth Taylor

*„Ich habe den Körper einer Frau und die Gefühle
eines Kindes."*
Elizabeth Taylor

« J'ai un corps de femme et un cœur d'enfant. »
Elizabeth Taylor

STILL FROM 'A DATE WITH JUDY' (1948)
Never one to deny herself anything, Carol (Elizabeth) tempts her more timid friend Judy (Jane Powell). / Carol (Elizabeth), die sich selbst nichts versagt, führt ihre etwas ängstlichere Freundin Judy (Jane Powell) in Versuchung. / Incapable de résister à la tentation, Carol (Elizabeth) essaie d'allécher sa timide amie Judy (Jane Powell).

PARTY (CIRCA 1949)
Rebellion begins. Partying with Hollywood girlfriends Jane Powell, Janet Leigh and Ann Blyth. / Der Beginn der Rebellion: Bei einer Party mit ihren Freundinnen aus Hollywood, Jane Powell, Janet Leigh und Ann Blyth. / Premiers signes de rébellion : Elizabeth fait la fête avec ses camarades d'Hollywood, Jane Powell, Janet Leigh et Ann Blyth.

STILL FROM 'JULIA MISBEHAVES' (1948)
Mother (Greer Garson) and daughter (Elizabeth) reunite. Elizabeth's relationship with her mother, Sara, was close but stifling. She was soon to rebel. / Mutter (Greer Garson) und Tochter (Elizabeth) sind wieder vereint. Elizabeths Beziehung zu ihrer Mutter Sara war eng, aber auch erdrückend. Bald würde sie aufsässig werden. / Retrouvailles entre la mère (Greer Garson) et la fille (Elizabeth). Étouffée par une relation trop fusionnelle avec sa mère Sara, la jeune actrice ne tardera pas à se rebeller.

STILL FROM 'LITTLE WOMEN' (1949)
Elizabeth begins to be cast as the spoiled daughter, here with Margaret O'Brien in director Mervyn LeRoy's deft adaptation. / Elizabeth spielt immer häufiger die Rolle der verwöhnten Tochter, hier mit Margaret O'Brien in der gelungenen Romanverfilmung von Mervyn LeRoy. / Ses premiers rôles d'enfant gâtée, ici aux côtés de Margaret O'Brien dans l'habile adaptation du réalisateur Mervyn LeRoy.

STILL FROM 'LITTLE WOMEN' (1949)
The "Little Women" gather around the much-awaited letter from father in this film about female solidarity under duress. / Die „jungen Frauen" sammeln sich, um einen langerwarteten Brief ihres Vaters zu lesen. / Les quatre filles du docteur March autour de la lettre de leur père, dans un film traitant de la solidarité féminine face à l'adversité.

PAGES 46/47
STILL FROM 'CONSPIRATOR' (1949)
Elizabeth is caught up in the anti-Red paranoia of the late 1940s in this mediocre spy thriller with Robert Taylor. / Elizabeth spielt eine Frau, die in die Paranoia um die „Rote Gefahr" Ende der vierziger Jahre verstrickt wird. / Elizabeth est entraînée dans la paranoïa anticommuniste de la fin des années 1940 dans ce médiocre thriller d'espionnage.

STILL FROM 'THE BIG HANGOVER' (1950)
This movie cannot decide whether it is a serious film noir or a comedy. Elizabeth's and Van Johnson's talents are squandered. / Dieser Film kann sich nicht entscheiden, ob er ein ernsthafter Film noir sein möchte oder eine Komödie. Die Talente von Elizabeth Taylor und Van Johnson wurden hier sinnlos vergeudet. / Hésitant entre le film noir et la comédie, ce film gaspille le talent de Liz Taylor et de Van Johnson.

ON THE SET OF 'FATHER OF THE BRIDE' (1950)
Art reflects life or vice-versa: Elizabeth was a bride on film while off-screen she was preparing to marry the first of a line of husbands: Nick Hilton. MGM even supplied her wedding dress. / Die Kunst spiegelt das Leben — oder umgekehrt: Elizabeth spielte im Film eine Braut, während sie sich privat auf die erste ihrer zahlreichen Ehen vorbereitete: mit Nick Hilton. MGM stellte sogar das Brautkleid zur Verfügung. / L'art est le reflet de la vie et vice versa : alors qu'elle incarne une mariée à l'écran, Elizabeth s'apprête à épouser Nick Hilton, le premier de ses nombreux maris. La MGM va jusqu'à fournir la robe.

PORTRAIT FOR 'FATHER'S LITTLE DIVIDEND' (1951)
Elizabeth in a portrait for the film; she was soon to have a "little dividend" of her own by second husband Michael Wilding. / Elizabeth in einem Porträt für den Film. Schon bald würde sie ihre eigene „kleine Dividende" (oder – gemäß dem deutschen Filmtitel – ihr eigenes „Geschenk des Himmels") in den Armen halten – von ihrem zweiten Ehemann, Michael Wilding. / Elizabeth, qui pose ici pour une photo promotionnelle, ne tardera pas à avoir un bébé à elle avec son deuxième époux, Michael Wilding.

STILL FROM 'FATHER'S LITTLE DIVIDEND' (1951)
Trying to recapture the success of 'Father of the Bride' by reuniting Spencer Tracy and Elizabeth with director Vincente Minnelli. / Die Fortsetzung versuchte, an den Erfolg von *Der Vater der Braut* anzuknüpfen, und brachte Spencer Tracy und Elizabeth Taylor erneut mit Regisseur Vincente Minnelli zusammen. / La MGM tente de recréer le succès du *Père de la mariée* en réunissant à nouveau Spencer Tracy, Elizabeth Taylor et le réalisateur Vincente Minnelli.

ON THE SET OF 'A PLACE IN THE SUN' (1951)
Director George Stevens (right) on location at Lake
Tahoe with Elizabeth; a brooding Montgomery Clift is
in the background. / Regisseur George Stevens (rechts)
bei Außenaufnahmen auf dem Lake Tahoe mit Elizabeth
— im Hintergrund ein grüblerischer Montgomery Clift. /
Aux côtés du réalisateur George Stevens lors du
tournage sur le lac Tahoe ; Montgomery Clift semble
songeur au second plan.

PORTRAIT FOR 'A PLACE IN THE SUN' (1951)
Elizabeth strikes a pose on the set. Would she still be
smiling if she knew that MGM charged Paramount
$35,000 for her services, when she only received
$10,000? / Elizabeth posiert während der Dreharbeiten.
Ob sie auch noch lächeln würde, wenn sie wüsste, dass
MGM von Paramount 35.000 Dollar für diese „Leih-
gabe" verlangte, von denen sie aber nur 10.000 erhielt? /
L'actrice photographiée sur le tournage serait-elle aussi
souriante si elle savait que la MGM a réclamé 35 000
dollars à la Paramount en échange de ses services, alors
qu'elle n'en touche que 10 000 ?

"I, along with the critics, have never taken myself very seriously."
Elizabeth Taylor

„Ich habe mich, genau wie die Kritiker, nie sonderlich ernst genommen."
Elizabeth Taylor

« Tout comme les critiques, je ne me suis jamais prise très au sérieux. »
Elizabeth Taylor

ON THE SET OF 'A PLACE IN THE SUN' (1951)
The cast and crew seem to be enjoying Shelley Winters' dunk in the water just a little too much. / Shelley Winters nimmt ein unfreiwilliges Bad im See, was ihren Kollegen und dem Stab offenbar schelmisches Vergnügen bereitet. / Les acteurs et les techniciens semblent se réjouir un peu trop du plongeon de Shelley Winter dans les eaux du lac.

ON THE SET OF 'A PLACE IN THE SUN' (1951)
George Stevens rehearses the landmark kiss. / George
Stevens bei den Proben zum legendären Kuss. / George
Stevens leur fait répéter le célèbre baiser.

STILL FROM 'A PLACE IN THE SUN' (1951)
The beginning of an intimate relationship with the
bisexual Montgomery Clift; all her life the motherly
Elizabeth found herself drawn to gay or bisexual
men. / Der Beginn einer intimen Beziehung zu dem
bisexuellen Montgomery Clift. Ihr ganzes Leben lang
fühlte sich die mütterliche Elizabeth zu homo- oder
bisexuellen Männern hingezogen. / Début d'une relation
intime avec le bisexuel Montgomery Clift; toute sa vie,
la très maternelle Elizabeth sera attirée par les hommes
homosexuels et bisexuels.

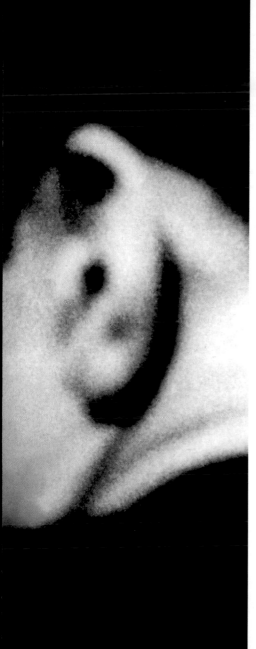

"When Monty Clift would start to shake, I would start to shake ... Only two actors I know [the other being Richard Burton] ... give to the degree that it's almost a physical thing, like an umbilical cord, an electricity that goes back and forth."
Elizabeth Taylor

„Wenn Monty Clift zu zittern begann, dann begann ich zu zittern ... Nur zwei Schauspieler, die ich kenne [der andere ist Richard Burton], ... spielen mit einer solchen Intensität, dass es fast schon eine körperliche Angelegenheit ist, wie eine Nabelschnur, ein Strom, der hin- und herfließt."
Elizabeth Taylor

« Quand Monty Clift commençait à trembler, je tremblais aussi ... Je ne connais que deux acteurs [l'autre étant Richard Burton] ... qui se donnent au point que c'en est presque physique, comme un cordon ombilical, un courant électrique qui circule de l'un à l'autre. »
Elizabeth Taylor

STILL FROM 'A PLACE IN THE SUN' (1951)
The kiss, an iconic creation of the American cinema. / Der Kuss gehört zu den ikonischen Kreationen des amerikanischen Kinos. / Le baiser, création emblématique du cinéma américain.

**STILL FROM 'LOVE IS BETTER THAN EVER'
(1952)**
Larry Parks, whose life and career will soon be
destroyed by the Blacklist, does not realize what he is in
for when dance teacher Elizabeth relentlessly pursues
him. / Larry Parks, dessen Leben und Karriere bald
durch die berüchtigten Schwarzen Listen zerstört
werden würde, weiß nicht, was ihm bevorsteht, als ihn
die Tanzlehrerin Stacie (Elizabeth Taylor) erbarmungslos
verfolgt. / Larry Parks, dont la vie et la carrière seront
bientôt anéanties par la chasse aux sorcières, ne se
doute pas de ce qui l'attend lorsque le professeur de
danse incarné par Elizabeth le poursuit de ses
assiduités.

"Her face is alive with youthful spirit, her voice has
the softness of sweet song and her whole manner is
one of refreshing grace."
Bosley Crowther, critic

„Ihr Gesicht sprüht vor jugendlichem Esprit, ihre
Stimme besitzt die Sanftheit eines süßen Gesangs,
und ihr ganzes Gebaren ist von erfrischender
Anmut."
Bosley Crowther, Kritiker

STILL FROM 'IVANHOE' (1952)
Elizabeth, whose mother was not on the set for the first
time in her career, epitomizes Sir Walter Scott's Jewish
heroine Rebecca. / Elizabeth, deren Mutter zum ersten
Mal in ihrer Karriere nicht bei den Dreharbeiten
anwesend war, ist die ideale Verkörperung von Sir
Walter Scotts jüdischer Heldin Rebecca. / Elizabeth,
dont la mère est absente du plateau pour la première
fois de sa carrière, incarne à la perfection Rebecca,
l'héroïne juive de Walter Scott.

« Son visage est animé d'un esprit juvénile, sa voix
est veloutée comme une chanson douce et tout son
être est empreint d'une grâce rafraîchissante. »
Bosley Crowther, critique

ABOVE/OBEN/CI-DESSUS
STILL FROM 'IVANHOE' (1952)
Robert Taylor as Ivanhoe tended to by Rebecca as they make up two sides of the romantic triangle central to the film. / Rebecca nimmt sich Ivanhoes (Robert Taylor) an. Das Paar bildet eine Seite der Dreiecksbeziehung, die im Mittelpunkt des Films steht. / Rebecca et Ivanhoé (Robert Taylor) forment deux côtés du triangle amoureux situé au centre de l'intrigue.

OPPOSITE/LINKS/CI-CONTRE
STILL FROM 'IVANHOE' (1952)
Rebecca ready to be martyred for her Jewish faith. / Rebecca ist bereit, für ihren jüdischen Glauben den Märtyrertod zu sterben. / Rebecca prête à endurer le martyre pour sa foi.

PAGES 64/65
STILL FROM 'THE GIRL WHO HAD EVERYTHING' (1953)
Elizabeth stars in a tepid remake of 'A Free Soul' (1931). She is caught between her sexual attraction to a gangster (Fernando Lamas) and her desire to please her lawyer father (William Powell). / Elizabeth spielt die Hauptrolle in diesem lauwarmen Aufguss von *Der Mut zum Glück* (1931). Sie ist gefangen zwischen ihrer sexuellen Anziehung zu einem Gangster (Fernando Lamas) und dem Wunsch nach Anerkennung durch ihren Vater (William Powell), einen Rechtsanwalt. / Dans un tiède remake d'*Âmes libres* (1931), dont l'héroïne est partagée entre son attirance pour un gangster (Fernando Lamas) et sa loyauté envers son avocat de père (William Powell).

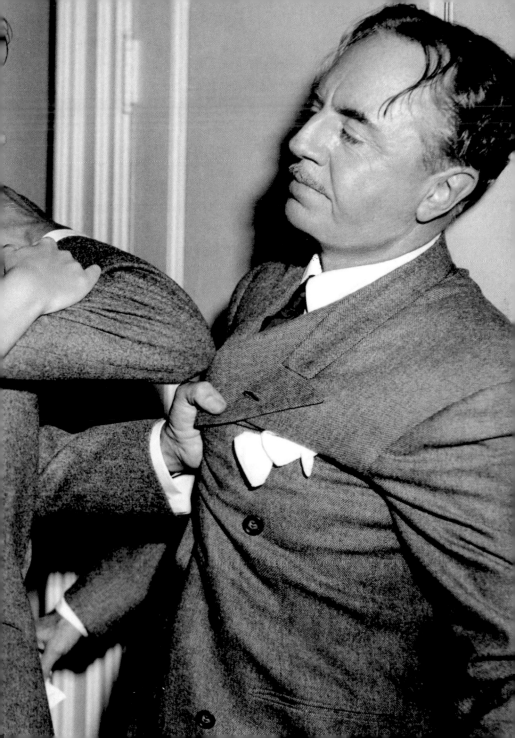

STILL FROM 'RHAPSODY' (1954)
Even after her success in 'A Place in the Sun' and
'Father of the Bride,' Elizabeth was still being miscast in
mediocre films. / Selbst nach ihrem Erfolg in *Eine
amerikanische Tragödie* und *Der Vater der Braut* wurde
Elizabeth noch immer in mittelmäßigen Filmen völlig
fehlbesetzt. / Même après le succès d'*Une place au
soleil* et du *Père de la mariée,* l'actrice continue d'être
mal employée dans des films médiocres.

STILL FROM 'RHAPSODY' (1954)
At least Italian actor Vittorio Gassman provided her
with the sexual energy she craved from her onscreen
co-stars. / Der italienische Schauspieler Vittorio
Gassman gab ihr wenigstens die sexuelle Energie, nach
der sie sich bei ihren Filmpartnern sehnte. / Du moins
l'acteur italien Vittorio Gassman lui apporte-t-il l'énergie
érotique qu'elle attend de ses partenaires à l'écran.

STILL FROM 'ELEPHANT WALK' (1954)
Elephants reclaim their traditional territory and destroy the plantation in an expensive film plagued by cost over-runs. / Elefanten erobern ihr angestammtes Terrain zurück und zerstören die Plantage in diesem teuren Film, dessen Kosten völlig aus dem Ruder liefen. / Les éléphants déterminés à reconquérir leur territoire détruisent la plantation dans cette production onéreuse grevée par les frais imprévus.

STILL FROM 'ELEPHANT WALK' (1954)
Replacing the ailing Vivien Leigh, Elizabeth injects her own full-bodied sexuality into the role of a woman frustrated by the distance of her psychologically conflicted husband (Peter Finch). / Als Ersatz für die erkrankte Vivien Leigh bringt Elizabeth mit vollem Körpereinsatz ihre eigene Sexualität in die Rolle einer Frau ein, die durch die Distanziertheit ihres geistig verwirrten Ehemanns (Peter Finch) frustriert ist. / Remplaçant Vivien Leigh, qui est souffrante, Elizabeth insuffle toute sa sensualité à son personnage de femme frustrée par la froideur de son mari (Peter Finch), en proie à des conflits intérieurs.

**STILL FROM 'THE LAST TIME I SAW PARIS'
(1954)**
Based on 'Babylon Revisited' by F. Scott Fitzgerald,
Helen (Elizabeth, here being charmed by Roger Moore)
is an echo of Fitzgerald's wife Zelda. / In Helen
(Elizabeth, hier mit einem charmanten Roger Moore)
findet man in dieser Verfilmung von F. Scott Fitzgeralds
Wiedersehen mit Babylon Anklänge an Fitzgeralds
Ehefrau Zelda. / Inspiré de la nouvelle de F. Scott
Fitzgerald *Retour à Babylone*, le personnage de Helen
(Elizabeth, ici courtisée par Roger Moore) rappelle
Zelda, l'épouse de l'écrivain.

STILL FROM 'BEAU BRUMMELL' (1954)
Stunningly beautiful as the courtesan Lady Patricia,
Elizabeth found the performance hilarious when she
watched it years later. / Obwohl sie als Kurtisane Lady
Patricia umwerfend schön war, fand Elizabeth ihr
Schauspiel lächerlich, als sie sich den Film Jahre später
noch einmal anschaute. / Somptueuse dans le rôle de
la courtisane Lady Patricia, Elizabeth trouvera son
interprétation hilarante lorsqu'elle la reverra des années
plus tard.

**STILL FROM 'THE LAST TIME I SAW PARIS'
(1954)**
Wearied, in love, and tormented: the writer (Van
Johnson) with his muse and wife, Helen. / Erschöpft,
verliebt und seelisch gequält: Der Schriftsteller (Van
Johnson) mit seiner Muse und Ehefrau Helen. / Las,
amoureux et tourmenté : l'écrivain (Van Johnson) avec
Helen, sa femme et sa muse.

PORTRAIT (1954)
Elizabeth exhibiting her zaftig figure, of which she was
never ashamed and which became the norm in 1950s
Hollywood. / Elizabeth stellt ihre üppigen Rundungen
zur Schau, für die sie sich nie schämte und die im
Hollywood der fünfziger Jahre zur Norm wurden. /
Elizabeth exhibe sa plantureuse silhouette dont elle
n'aura jamais honte et qui deviendra la norme à
Hollywood dans les années 1950.

ON THE SET OF 'GIANT' (1956)
Elizabeth reunited with director George Stevens, in cowboy hat, for another landmark film. Here she is with co-star Rock Hudson, another closeted gay man who became a lifelong friend. / Elizabeth war wieder mit Regisseur George Stevens (im Cowboyhut) vereint, um einen weiteren bahnbrechenden Film zu drehen. Hier ist sie mit ihrem Kollegen Rock Hudson zu sehen, einem weiteren heimlichen Homosexuellen, mit dem sie sein ganzes Leben lang befreundet blieb. / Elizabeth retrouve le réalisateur George Stevens (en chapeau de cow-boy) pour un autre film marquant. Elle se tient ici aux côtés de son partenaire Rock Hudson, autre homosexuel refoulé qui restera son ami.

STILL FROM 'GIANT' (1956)
Elizabeth plays a girl from the East who fights the deep-seated racial intolerance of Texas, a sentiment that echoes Elizabeth's views on homosexuality. / Elizabeth spielt ein Mädchen aus dem Osten, das gegen die tiefverwurzelte Rassenintoleranz in Texas ankämpft — eine Haltung, in der sich Elizabeths Ansichten zur Homosexualität spiegeln. / L'actrice, qui lutte contre la discrimination envers les homosexuels, combat dans ce film une autre forme d'intolérance : le racisme profondément enraciné au Texas.

ON THE SET OF 'GIANT' (1956)

James Dean tried to charm Elizabeth away from Rock Hudson, playing out the film story in real life. / James Dean versuchte, Elizabeth mit seinem Charme von Rock Hudson fortzulocken, womit er die Filmhandlung im wahren Leben nachahmte. / Transposant l'intrigue du film dans la vraie vie, James Dean tente de ravir Elizabeth à Rock Hudson.

ON THE SET OF 'GIANT' (1956)

Her relationship with James Dean ran hot and cold — he would spend long nights talking intimately about himself, then freeze out Elizabeth, thinking he had revealed too much. / Ihre Beziehung zu James Dean hatte Höhen und Tiefen. Er verbrachte ganze Nächte damit, ihr seine Seele auszuschütten, und ging Elizabeth dann völlig aus dem Weg, weil er fürchtete, ihr gegenüber zuviel von sich preisgegeben zu haben. / Avec elle, James Dean souffle le chaud et le froid : après avoir passé des nuits entières à lui confier ses pensées intimes, il devient soudain glacial, regrettant d'en avoir trop dit.

**COSTUME TEST FOR 'RAINTREE COUNTY'
(1957)**
Elizabeth moves with ease into the role of the
psychologically disturbed femme fatale Susanna Drake,
which earned her an Oscar nomination. / Elizabeth
konnte sich leicht in die Rolle der geistig verwirrten
Femme fatale Susanna Drake hineinversetzen und
wurde dafür mit einer „Oscar"-Nominierung belohnt. /
Elizabeth s'installe sans peine dans le rôle de Susanna
Drake, femme fatale à la psychologie instable, qui lui
vaudra une nomination aux Oscars.

STILL FROM 'RAINTREE COUNTY' (1957)
Sharing many characteristics with Scarlett O'Hara,
Elizabeth pulls out all the stops in her performance as
the Southern Belle of the film, even though the tight
corsets caused her to hyperventilate. / Elizabeth, die
Scarlett O'Hara in vielerlei Hinsicht ähnelte, geht in
ihrer Darstellung der Südstaatenschönheit aufs Ganze,
wenngleich ihr das enge Korsett mitunter die Luft
nahm. / Partageant de nombreux points communs avec
Scarlett O'Hara, Elizabeth se lâche totalement dans le
rôle de cette héroïne sudiste, même si son terrible
corset la laisse au bord de l'asphyxie.

"Bessie Mae [Elizabeth] is the only person I know who has more wrong with her than I have. Tragedies are not cathartic. They make life more mysterious."
Montgomery Clift

„Bessie Mae [Elizabeth] ist die einzige Person, die ich kenne, bei der noch weniger stimmt als bei mir selbst. Tragödien bieten keine Katharsis. Sie machen das Leben geheimnisvoller."
Montgomery Clift

« Bessie Mae [Elizabeth] est la seule personne de ma connaissance qui a plus de problèmes que moi. Les tragédies ne sont pas cathartiques. Elles rendent la vie plus mystérieuse. »
Montgomery Clift

OPPOSITE/LINKS/CI-CONTRE
STILL FROM 'RAINTREE COUNTY' (1957)
In this antiwar and antiracism film, Montgomery Clift plays an idealistic Indiana man whose wife (Elizabeth Taylor) becomes progressively insane. / In diesem Film gegen Krieg und Rassismus spielt Montgomery Clift einen Idealisten aus Indiana, dessen Ehefrau (Elizabeth Taylor) immer mehr dem Wahnsinn anheimfällt. / Dans ce film contre la guerre et le racisme, Montgomery Clift incarne un idéaliste dont l'épouse (Elizabeth Taylor) perd peu à peu la raison.

PAGE 82
STILL FROM 'RAINTREE COUNTY' (1957)
The rapport between the leads radiates from the screen. Clift was Elizabeth's best friend and mentor. / Die Harmonie zwischen den beiden Hauptdarstellern ist auch im Kinosaal spürbar. Clift war Elizabeths bester Freund und Mentor. / La complicité qui unit les deux acteurs est palpable à l'écran. Clift est le meilleur ami et le mentor d'Elizabeth.

PAGE 83
ON THE SET OF 'RAINTREE COUNTY' (1957)
On the set, Elizabeth was word-perfect, on-time, unassuming, genial, and good fun. / Bei den Dreharbeiten kannte Elizabeth ihren Text aufs Wort genau, war pünktlich, anspruchslos, jovial und immer zu Späßen aufgelegt. / L'actrice, qui sait son texte sur le bout des doigts, se montre toujours ponctuelle, modeste, chaleureuse et drôle.

LA GATTA
SULTETTO
CHE SCOTTA
(CAT ON A HOT TIN ROOF)

**PORTRAIT FOR 'CAT ON A HOT TIN ROOF'
(1958)**
Tennessee Williams' sexually charged play centers on
Maggie "the Cat." / Das sexuell aufgeladene Stück von
Tennessee Williams dreht sich um „die Katze" Maggie. /
La pièce à forte connotation érotique de Tennessee
Williams est centrée sur le personnage de Maggie.

**POSTER FOR 'CAT ON A HOT TIN ROOF'
(1958)**
Italian artwork for the movie. / Italienisches
Werbeplakat für den Film. / L'affiche italienne du film.

ON THE SET OF 'CAT ON A HOT TIN ROOF'
(1958)
Burl Ives, who plays Big Daddy, pays homage to the
megastar. / Burl Ives, der Big Daddy spielt, erweist dem
Megastar seine Ehre. / Burl Ives, qui interprète Big
Daddy, présente ses hommages à la star.

STILL FROM 'CAT ON A HOT TIN ROOF' (1958)
Here caressing her leg while her crippled husband
(Paul Newman) watches in a combination of disgust and
fear. His broken leg is an allegory for his guilt and
impotence. / Hier streichelt sie ihr Bein, während ihr
verletzter Ehemann (Paul Newman) ihr halb verängstigt,
halb angewidert zuschaut. Sein gebrochenes Bein ist
eine Metapher für seine Schuld und seine Impotenz. /
Maggie se caresse le mollet sous le regard à la fois
dégoûté et craintif de son mari (Paul Newman), dont la
jambe cassée est un symbole de culpabilité et
d'impuissance.

**STILL FROM 'SUDDENLY, LAST SUMMER'
(1959)**

An iconic photo of Elizabeth in her prime as Tennessee Williams' sexually charged Catherine; she is being used by Sebastian to lure young men. / Ein ikonisches Foto von Elizabeth in ihrer Blütezeit als sexuell aufgeladene Catherine im Stück von Tennessee Williams. Sebastian nutzt sie aus, um junge Männer anzulocken. / Image emblématique d'Elizabeth à la fleur de l'âge dans le rôle de Catherine, la voluptueuse héroïne de Tennessee Williams, que son cousin utilise pour attirer les jeunes gens.

**STILL FROM 'SUDDENLY, LAST SUMMER'
(1959)**

Alternating between femme fatale and victim, Elizabeth draws on the mounting tragedy in her own life, including the death of husband Mike Todd and the brutality of the scandal press. / Beim Wechsel zwischen Femme fatale und Opfer schöpft Elizabeth ihre Inspiration aus der wachsenden Tragik ihres Privatlebens, wo sie sowohl den Tod ihres Ehemanns Mike Todd als auch die Unbarmherzigkeit der Journaille verkraften muss. / Alternant entre la femme fatale et la victime, l'actrice puise dans son existence de plus en plus tragique, marquée par la mort de son mari Mike Todd et la brutalité de la presse à scandale.

**ON THE SET OF 'SUDDENLY, LAST SUMMER'
(1959)**
The cast (Hepburn, Clift, Taylor) and director
(Mankiewicz) confirm rumors of discord on the set. /
Die Darsteller (Hepburn, Clift, Taylor) und der Regisseur
(Mankiewicz) „bestätigen" Gerüchte über Dissonanzen
bei den Dreharbeiten. / Les acteurs (Hepburn, Clift,
Taylor) et le réalisateur (Mankiewicz) corroborent les
rumeurs faisant état de dissensions sur le tournage.

PAGE 92
**ON THE SET OF 'SUDDENLY, LAST SUMMER'
(1959)**
An exhausted yet still supremely erotic Elizabeth
suffers the Spanish sun. / Eine erschöpfte und trotzdem
noch äußerst erotische Elizabeth leidet unter der Sonne
Spaniens. / Somptueusement érotique malgré son
régime draconien, l'actrice s'offre au soleil d'Espagne.

**ON THE SET OF 'SUDDENLY, LAST SUMMER'
(1959)**
Elizabeth radiates a darkness and complexity which
enriches the character of Catherine. / Elizabeth strahlt
eine Düsterkeit und Komplexität aus, die die Figur der
Catherine bereichert. / Il émane d'Elizabeth une
ténébreuse complexité qui enrichit le personnage de
Catherine.

PAGE 93
**ON THE SET OF 'SUDDENLY, LAST SUMMER'
(1959)**
And yet the next moment she is filled with life as the
cameras roll. / Im nächsten Augenblick stand sie wieder
quicklebendig auf den Beinen. / L'instant d'après, elle
redevient pétillante de vie sous l'œil de la caméra.

STILL FROM 'BUTTERFIELD 8' (1960)
Venus in furs: MGM capitalizes on Elizabeth's 'bad girl' image and even casts Eddie Fisher, the man she 'stole' from actress Debbie Reynolds, in a role. / Venus im Pelz: MGM schlug aus Elizabeths Image als „schlimmes Mädchen" Kapital und gab sogar Eddie Fisher – dem Mann, den sie ihrer Kollegin Debbie Reynolds abspenstig gemacht hatte – eine Rolle in diesem Film. / Vénus au vison : la MGM exploite son image de « mauvaise fille » et confie même un rôle à Eddie Fisher, l'homme qu'elle a « volé » à l'actrice Debbie Reynolds.

STILL FROM 'BUTTERFIELD 8' (1960)
Elizabeth only made the film to complete her obligations to the studio, but it paid off for her big time: she finally received an Oscar after three nominations in a row. / Elizabeth drehte diesen Film nur, um ihren Vertrag mit dem Studio zu erfüllen, aber er zahlte sich prächtig für sie aus: Nach drei aufeinander folgenden Nominierungen wurde sie nun endlich mit einem „Oscar" ausgezeichnet. / Bien qu'elle n'ait accepté ce rôle que par obligation envers le studio, elle sera largement récompensée en recevant enfin un oscar après trois nominations de suite.

STILL FROM 'CLEOPATRA' (1963)
Elizabeth as the most famous femme fatale of all time,
Cleopatra, who 'conquers' Julius Caesar (Rex Harrison)
so that together they can bring peace to the world. /
Elizabeth als berühmteste Femme fatale aller Zeiten:
Kleopatra, die Julius Caesar (Rex Harrison) „erobert",
damit sie der Welt gemeinsam Frieden bringen
können. / Dans le rôle de Cléopâtre, la femme fatale
la plus célèbre de tous les temps, qui va « conquérir »
Jules César (Rex Harrison) pour rétablir la paix dans
le monde.

*"If someone's dumb enough to offer me a million
dollars to make a picture, I'm certainly not dumb
enough to turn it down."*
Elizabeth Taylor

*„Wenn jemand dumm genug ist, mir eine Million
Dollar zu bieten, um einen Film zu drehen, dann
bin ich gewiss nicht dumm genug, das Angebot
abzulehnen."*
Elizabeth Taylor

*« Si quelqu'un est assez bête pour m'offrir
un million de dollars pour faire un film, je ne suis
certainement pas assez bête pour le refuser. »*
Elizabeth Taylor

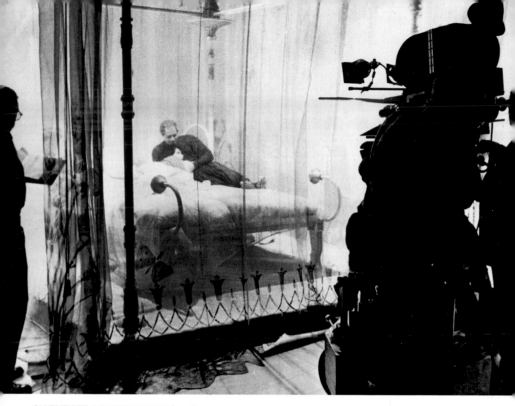

ON THE SET OF 'CLEOPATRA' (1963)
Filming began in England, with director Rouben
Mamoulian, many different cast members and huge
sets. Everything was scrapped and refilmed in Rome
with new writer/director Joseph L. Mankiewicz. /
Die Dreharbeiten begannen in England mit Rouben
Mamoulian als Regisseur, einer ganz anderen Besetzung
und gewaltigen Kulissen. All das wurde aber verworfen
und in Rom neu gedreht, diesmal nach dem Buch und
unter der Regie von Joseph L. Mankiewicz. /
Commencé en Angleterre avec une distribution
différente, d'immenses décors et le réalisateur Rouben
Mamoulian, le tournage redémarre à zéro, à Rome,
avec le scénariste et metteur en scène Joseph L.
Mankiewicz.

PAGES 98/99
ON THE SET OF 'CLEOPATRA' (1963)
The pharoah/queen of Egypt enters Rome in a
spectacle rarely equaled in the history of cinema. /
Die Pharaonin/Königin von Ägypten hält mit einem
Spektakel, das in der Geschichte des Kinos kaum
seinesgleichen finden dürfte, Einzug in Rom. / L'arrivée
à Rome de la reine d'Égypte, dans un spectacle
rarement égalé dans l'histoire du cinéma.

STILL FROM 'CLEOPATRA' (1963)
Hoping to claim through her son by Caeser her place on the throne of Rome, Cleopatra wows even the blasé Romans. / Mit ihrem Anspruch auf den römischen Kaiserthron durch ihren und Caesars gemeinsamen Sohn verblüfft Kleopatra sogar die blasierten Römer. / Espérant obtenir une place sur le trône de Rome par le biais du fils qu'elle a eu avec César, Cléopâtre époustoufle même les plus blasés des Romains.

STILL FROM 'CLEOPATRA' (1963)
Director Mankiewicz underpinned the epic arc of the story with honest human emotion. Here, Cleopatra winks at Caesar, implying 'How's that for an entrance?' / Regisseur Mankiewicz untermauerte den epischen Erzählbogen mit wahrhaftigen menschlichen Gefühlen. Hier blinzelt Kleopatra Caesar zu, als wolle sie sagen: „Na, was hältst du von diesem Auftritt?" / Mankiewicz laisse percer sous l'éclat épique de l'intrigue la chaleur des sentiments humains. Le clin d'œil que Cléopâtre adresse ici à César semble dire : « Que dis-tu de ça ? »

STILL FROM 'CLEOPATRA' (1963)
Richard Burton and Elizabeth Taylor had their first
scene together on 22 January 1962. Producer Walter
Wanger: 'You could almost feel the electricity between
Liz and Burton.' / Richard Burton und Elizabeth Taylor
drehten ihre erste gemeinsame Szene am 22. Januar
1962. Produzent Walter Wanger: „Man konnte das
Knistern zwischen Liz und Burton fast spüren." /
Richard Burton et Elizabeth Taylor tournent pour la
première fois ensemble le 22 janvier 1962. Selon le
producteur Walter Wanger, « le courant qui passait
entre eux était presque palpable ».

STILL FROM 'CLEOPATRA' (1963)
After the death of Caesar, Cleopatra persuades her
first love, Marc Antony, to fight Rome to unite the world.
But Marc Antony proves unequal to the task. / Nach
Caesars Tod überredet Kleopatra ihre erste Liebe,
Mark Anton, gegen Rom zu kämpfen, um die Welt zu
einen, aber es erweist sich, dass Mark Anton der
Aufgabe nicht gewachsen ist. / Après la mort de César,
Cléopâtre persuade Marc Antoine, son premier amour,
de combattre Rome pour unifier le monde. Mais il ne
se montre pas à la hauteur.

STILL FROM 'THE V.I.P.s' (1963)
Now married, the Burtons begin a series of movies in
which their personal and public angst is played out on
screen, here with Louis Jourdan. / Nachdem sie nun
verheiratet waren, begannen die Burtons eine Reihe
von Filmen zu drehen, in denen sie ihre private und
öffentliche Lebensangst auch auf die Leinwand
brachten, hier mit Louis Jourdan. / Désormais mariés,
les Burton entament une série de films où leurs
problèmes publics et privés s'affichent à l'écran,
comme ici avec Louis Jourdan.

*"[Burton] was poisoned by guilt: equally, he was
obsessed by [Elizabeth], who brought out the finest
and the most destructive forces in him."*
Melvyn Bragg, biographer

*„[Burton] war von Schuld vergiftet: Er war aber
gleichermaßen von [Elizabeth] besessen, die die
besten und die zerstörerischsten Kräfte in ihm
freisetzte."*
Melvyn Bragg, Biograph

STILL FROM 'THE V.I.P.s' (1963)
The jealous husband punishes the cheating wife.
Elizabeth now had complete control of her image,
with approval on photos, make-up, hair, costumes,
script, director, and even which takes to print. /
Der eifersüchtige Ehemann bestraft die untreue Frau.
Elizabeth besaß nun die volle Kontrolle über ihr Image
und musste um ihr Einverständnis gefragt werden,
wenn es um Fotos, Maske, Frisur, Drehbuch und Regie
ging und sogar darum, welche Aufnahmen im Film
verwendet wurden und welche nicht. / La femme
infidèle punie par le mari jaloux. L'actrice, qui contrôle
désormais son image, a son mot à dire sur les photos,
les costumes, les coiffures, le maquillage, le scénario,
le réalisateur et même le choix des prises.

« [Burton] était à la fois torturé par la
culpabilité et obsédé par [Elizabeth], qui faisait
ressortir les forces les plus remarquables et les
plus destructrices qu'il avait en lui. »
Melvyn Bragg, biographe

ON THE SET OF 'BECKET' (1964)

When not working on her own films, Elizabeth visits her husband on set, here in costume as an extra surprising Richard and Peter O'Toole. / Wenn sie nicht an eigenen Filmen arbeitete, besuchte Elizabeth ihren Ehemann bei seinen Dreharbeiten. Hier überrascht sie Richard Burton und Peter O'Toole als Statistin im Kostüm. / Lorsqu'elle ne tourne pas, Elizabeth rend visite à son mari sur les plateaux, ici dans un costume de figurante qui surprend Richard et Peter O'Toole.

"You find out who your real friends are when you're involved in a scandal."
Elizabeth Taylor

„Wenn du in einen Skandal verwickelt bist, dann findest du heraus, wer deine wirklichen Freunde sind."
Elizabeth Taylor

« On reconnaît ses vrais amis quand on est impliqué dans un scandale. »
Elizabeth Taylor

STILL FROM 'THE SANDPIPER' (1965)
Elizabeth reunites with director Vincente Minnelli in this overheated melodrama of art, sex, and religion as the couple continue to shock the public on and off screen. / Elizabeth arbeitete in diesem überhitzten Melodram über Kunst, Sex und Religion erneut mit Regisseur Vincente Minnelli zusammen, während das Ehepaar weiterhin auf der Leinwand wie auch im Leben öffentliche Entrüstung provozierte. / Elizabeth retrouve Vincente Minnelli dans ce mélodrame surchauffé où le couple, qui continue à choquer le public à la ville comme à l'écran, évoque l'art, le sexe et la religion.

**REHEARSAL FOR 'WHO'S AFRAID OF
VIRGINIA WOOLF?' (1966)**
The domineering Elizabeth seems to enjoy this part
of the rehearsal a little too much, with director Mike
Nichols. / Die herrische Elizabeth — mit Regisseur Mike
Nichols — scheint diesen Teil der Proben ein wenig zu
sehr zu genießen. / Très dominatrice, Elizabeth semble
particulièrement apprécier cette séance de répétition
aux côtés du réalisateur Mike Nichols.

**STILL FROM 'WHO'S AFRAID OF VIRGINIA
WOOLF?' (1966)**
Elizabeth gives her most abusive, strident performance
as Martha in Edward Albee's classic play and wins
another Oscar. / Nie war Elizabeth ausfallender und
schriller als in der Rolle der Martha in Edward Albees
Bühnenklassiker, und erneut erhielt sie einen „Oscar". /
Elizabeth signe son interprétation la plus agressive et la
plus virulente dans le rôle de Martha, l'héroïne de la
célèbre pièce d'Edward Albee, qui lui vaut un nouvel
oscar.

STILL FROM 'WHO'S AFRAID OF VIRGINIA WOOLF?' (1966)
Seductive even as a zaftig middle-aged shrew, Martha puts the moves on a young academic (George Segal). / Selbst als mollige Schreckschraube mittleren Alters macht sich die verführerische Martha noch an einen jungen Akademiker (George Segal) heran. / Séduisante même dans le rôle d'une plantureuse harpie, elle jette son dévolu sur un jeune universitaire (George Segal).

"Success is a great deodorant. It takes away all your past smells."
Elizabeth Taylor

„Erfolg ist ein großartiges Deodorant. Es entfernt alle Gerüche der Vergangenheit."
Elizabeth Taylor

« Le succès est un merveilleux déodorant. Il détruit toutes les vieilles odeurs. »
Elizabeth Taylor

STILL FROM 'WHO'S AFRAID OF VIRGINIA WOOLF?' (1966)
The submissive object of Martha's abuse (Burton) thinks about taking revenge, to no avail. / Das unterwürfige Opfer von Marthas Beschimpfungen (Burton) denkt an Rache — aber es bleibt beim Gedanken. / Le mari soumis (Burton) qui subit les injures de Martha rêve un instant de se venger, mais en vain.

STILL FROM 'WHO'S AFRAID OF VIRGINIA WOOLF?' (1966)
Elizabeth and director Nichols worked compulsively to shape the "virago" that Elizabeth played. / Elizabeth und Regisseur Nichols arbeiteten wie besessen daran, die Figur der „Xanthippe", die Elizabeth spielte, herauszuarbeiten. / L'actrice et le réalisateur Mike Nichols travaillent d'arrache-pied pour façonner ce personnage de furie.

"I feel very adventurous. There are so many doors to be opened, and I'm not afraid to look behind them."
Elizabeth Taylor

„Ich fühle mich sehr abenteuerlustig. Es gibt noch so viele Türen, die zu öffnen sind, und ich habe keine Angst, dahinter zu schauen."
Elizabeth Taylor

STILL FROM 'WHO'S AFRAID OF VIRGINIA WOOLF?' (1966)
Elizabeth altered her voice, was aged using makeup, gained weight and performed physically dangerous stunts. / Elizabeth verstellte ihre Stimme, wurde durch die Maske gealtert, nahm zu und vollführte einige Stunts selbst, bei denen sie sich leicht hätte verletzen können. / Pour ce rôle, Elizabeth change de voix, prend du poids, se vieillit à coup de maquillage et effectue de périlleuses cascades.

« J'ai l'esprit d'aventure. Il y a tant de portes à ouvrir, je n'ai pas peur de regarder ce qu'il y a derrière. »
Elizabeth Taylor

STILL FROM 'WHO'S AFRAID OF VIRGINIA WOOLF?' (1966)
Elizabeth managed to outshine her Shakespearean-trained husband and prove her own worth as an actress. / Elizabeth schaffte es, ihren durch Shakespeare-Rollen geschulten Ehemann an die Wand zu spielen, und zeigte, dass sie schauspielerisch auf eigenen Beinen stehen konnte. / Elizabeth parvient à éclipser son mari, acteur shakespearien, et à prouver son propre talent d'actrice.

"I am a very committed wife. And I should be committed too — for being married so many times."
Elizabeth Taylor

„Ich bin eine sehr engagierte Ehefrau, und ich sollte eingewiesen werden — weil ich so oft verheiratet war."
Elizabeth Taylor

« Je suis une épouse hors normes. D'ailleurs, il ne faut pas être normal pour se marier autant de fois. »
Elizabeth Taylor

STILL FROM 'WHO'S AFRAID OF VIRGINIA WOOLF?' (1966)
The film is Elizabeth's 'coming of age' as an actress according to biographer Alexander Walker. / Der Film war ihrem Biographen Alexander Walker zufolge Elizabeths schauspielerische „Reifeprüfung". / Selon le biographe Alexander Walker, c'est avec ce film qu'elle « parvient à maturité » en tant que comédienne.

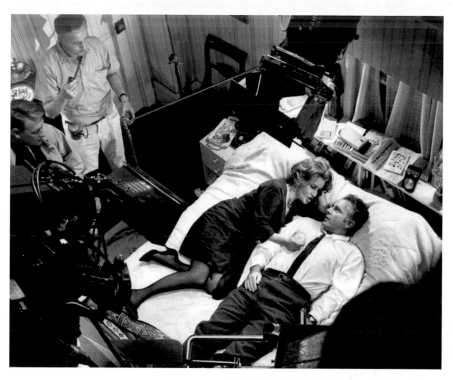

ON THE SET OF 'WHO'S AFRAID OF VIRGINIA WOOLF?' (1966)
Elizabeth: "I'm wonderful at playing bitches." So good, in fact, that she became typecast. / Elizabeth: „Ich kann wunderbar Zicken spielen." So gut sogar, dass man sie bei der Rollenvergabe in eine entsprechende Schublade steckte. / « Je suis parfaite pour jouer les garces », avoue Elizabeth, qui se retrouvera d'ailleurs enfermée dans ce rôle.

STILL FROM 'WHO'S AFRAID OF VIRGINIA WOOLF?' (1966)
In the end, despite the battles and insults and hurt that these two wounded souls have wrought upon themselves, the bond of mutual tenderness is revealed momentarily. / Am Ende schimmern — trotz aller Kämpfe, die diese beiden verletzten Seelen untereinander ausgetragen haben, und der Beleidigungen, die sie sich gegenseitig an den Kopf warfen — für einen kurzen Augenblick die Bande der Zärtlichkeit durch. / Malgré les insultes et la peine que se sont infligées ces deux écorchés vifs, leur tendresse mutuelle réapparaît brièvement à la fin.

118

STILL FROM 'THE TAMING OF THE SHREW' (1967)
Elizabeth reprises her role from 'Who's Afraid of Virginia Woolf?' but with a Shakespearean touch. / Sie spielt die gleiche Rolle wie in *Wer hat Angst vor Virginia Woolf?*, diesmal mit einem Hauch von Shakespeare. / Elizabeth reprend le rôle de *Qui a peur de Virginia Woolf?*, une touche shakespearienne en plus.

PAGES 120/121
STILL FROM 'THE TAMING OF THE SHREW' (1967)
Petruchio learns the hard way that you can never really conquer a dominant woman, even with a bridal veil. / Petruchio lernt auf schmerzhafte Art, dass man eine dominante Frau niemals zähmen kann. / Petruchio sait qu'on ne peut jamais dompter une femme dominatrice, même avec un voile de mariée.

POSTER FOR 'THE TAMING OF THE SHREW' (1967)
This Spanish poster adds a whip for Petruchio to tame Katharina. / Auf dem spanischen Filmplakat hat man Petruchio noch eine Peitsche in die Hand gedrückt, um Katharina zu zähmen. / Cette affiche espagnole affuble Petruchio d'un fouet pour apprivoiser la mégère.

STILL FROM 'THE TAMING OF THE SHREW' (1967)
Elizabeth always enjoyed physicality in all its forms even though she paid for it all her life, with various ailments. / Trotz andauernden Leiden genoss Elizabeth das Körperliche voll und ganz. / Elizabeth apprécie la physicalité sous toutes ses formes, même au prix de problèmes de santé permanents.

PAGE 125
ON THE SET OF 'THE TAMING OF THE SHREW' (1967)
Although she demanded respect and adoration, she also gave the young director her best. / Obwohl sie Respekt und Verehrung erwartete, gab sie dem jungen Regisseur auch ihrerseits ihr Bestes. / Bien qu'elle exige le respect et l'adoration, elle donne au jeune réalisateur le meilleur d'elle-même.

STILL FROM 'THE TAMING OF THE SHREW' (1967)
Elizabeth deferred payment on this film because she believed in it. / Elizabeth ließ die Gage in diesem Fall erst nachträglich auszahlen, weil sie an das Projekt glaubte. / La star croit assez en ce film pour différer le versement de son cachet.

PAGE 124
ON THE SET OF 'THE TAMING OF THE SHREW' (1967)
Elizabeth, ever the diva, expected homage from director Franco Zeffirelli, including jewels. He delivered. / Die Diva Elizabeth erwartete von Regisseur Franco Zeffirelli Huldigung, auch in Form von Schmuck. / Éternelle diva, Elizabeth s'attend à ce que le réalisateur Franco Zeffirelli se prosterne devant elle et la couvre de bijoux. Elle sera servie.

STILL FROM 'THE TAMING OF THE SHREW' (1967)
In the end Petruchio tames Katharina, and vice versa. Such was not the case for the real-life couple. / Am Ende zähmt Petruchio Katharina — und umgekehrt. Im Privatleben des Ehepaars sah es anders aus. / Petruchio finit par apprivoiser Katharina, et réciproquement. On ne peut en dire autant du couple qu'ils forment dans la vraie vie.

STILL FROM 'THE TAMING OF THE SHREW' (1967)
During the production, Elizabeth received the news of Montgomery Clift's death, then gave one of her funniest scenes. / Während der Dreharbeiten erfuhr Elizabeth von Montgomery Clifts Tod und spielte anschließend eine ihrer lustigsten Szenen. / Durant le tournage, Elizabeth apprend la mort de Montgomery Clift juste avant de jouer l'une de ses scènes les plus drôles.

ABOVE/OBEN/CI-DESSUS
STILL FROM 'DOCTOR FAUSTUS' (1967)
Demonstrating that Elizabeth still had sex appeal, she
appears as the ideal of beauty, Helen of Troy. / Um zu
beweisen, dass sie noch immer Sex-Appeal besaß,
spielte Elizabeth das Schönheitsideal Helena von
Troja. / Démontrant qu'elle n'a rien perdu de son
sex-appeal, elle incarne un idéal de beauté, Hélène
de Troie.

OPPOSITE/RECHTS/CI-CONTRE
STILL FROM 'DOCTOR FAUSTUS' (1967)
Faustus (nor Burton?) cannot help but sell his soul for
a taste of her. / Faustus (Burton) kommt nicht umhin,
seine Seele zu verkaufen, um von ihr zu „kosten". /
Faust (comme Burton ?) ne peut s'empêcher de vendre
son âme par amour pour la belle.

PAGES 130/131
STILL FROM 'REFLECTIONS IN A GOLDEN EYE' (1967)
Maj. Weldon Penderton, a closeted gay army officer (Marlon Brando in a part designed for Montgomery Clift), is the object of abuse for his sexually frustrated wife Leonora. / Major Weldon Penderton, ein insgeheim homosexueller Offizier (Marlon Brando in einer für Montgomery Clift geschriebenen Rolle), wird von seiner sexuell frustrierten Ehefrau Leonora beschimpft. / Homosexuel refoulé, le major Weldon Penderton (Marlon Brando dans un rôle conçu pour Montgomery Clift) se fait incendier par Leonora, son épouse frustrée.

RICHARD BURTON - ELIZABETH TAYLOR
ALEC GUINNESS - PETER USTINOV

I COMMEDIANTI
(THE COMEDIANS)

DAL ROMANZO DI **GRAHAM GREENE**   con **PAUL FORD - LILLIAN GISH**
EDITO IN ITALIA DA MONDADORI

SCENEGGIATURA DI **GRAHAM GREENE**   PRODOTTO E DIRETTO DA **PETER GLENVILLE**   in **PANAVISION**™ **METROCOLOR**

AVVERTENZA

STILL FROM 'THE COMEDIANS' (1967)
The Burtons cannot stop working, loving, or fighting, often all at the same time. / Die Burtons konnten nicht aufhören zu arbeiten, sich zu lieben oder sich zu streiten – und das oft alles gleichzeitig. / Les Burton ne cessent de travailler, de s'aimer ou de se disputer, voire les trois à la fois.

PAGES 134/135
ADVERT FOR 'THE COMEDIANS' (1967)
Artwork for the film adapted from Graham Greene's novel. / Werbung für den Film nach dem Roman von Graham Greene. / Publicité pour le film adapté du roman de Graham Greene.

POSTER FOR 'THE COMEDIANS' (1967)
The Italian poster. Elizabeth always undervalued her own skills: "I am just a broad, but Richard is a great actor." / Das italienische Filmplakat. Elizabeth spielte ihr eigenes Talent immer herunter: „Ich bin nur ein Weibsstück, aber Richard ist ein großartiger Schauspieler." / L'affiche italienne du film. Elizabeth sous-estimera toujours son propre talent : « Je ne suis qu'une nana, mais Richard est un grand acteur. »

They lie, they cheat,

STILL FROM 'BOOM' (1968)
Tennessee Williams adapted his play 'The Milk Train
Doesn't Stop Here Anymore' for the screen and for
Elizabeth's persona. / Tennessee Williams schrieb das
Drehbuch nach seinem Theaterstück *Der Milchzug hält
hier nicht mehr* und schnitt es auf Elizabeth zu. /
Tennessee Williams adapte sa pièce *Le train de l'aube
ne s'arrête plus ici* pour le cinéma en pensant à Liz
Taylor.

STILL FROM 'BOOM' (1968)
The Burtons formed a creative relationship with
blacklisted American director Joseph Losey. Elizabeth
plays the lonely but rich Flora Goforth, here pictured
with the Witch of Capri, played by Noel Coward. / Die
Burtons arbeiten schöpferisch mit dem amerikanischen
Regisseur Joseph Losey zusammen, der in seiner
Heimat auf den Schwarzen Listen stand. Elizabeth
spielt die einsame, aber reiche Flora Goforth, hier im
Bild mit der „Hexe von Capri", gespielt von Noel
Coward. / Les Burton nouent une relation fructueuse
avec le réalisateur américain Joseph Losey, placé sur
liste noire. Elizabeth incarne la riche et solitaire Flora
Goforth, ici aux côtés du « sorcier de Capri », interprété
par Noel Coward.

STILL FROM 'BOOM' (1968)
Burton, in the samurai costume, feared he was a little
too old for the "beautiful" poet. And Elizabeth looked
too healthy for the frail, dying Flora. / Burton — im
Samuraikostüm — befürchtete, er sei für die Rolle des
„schönen" Dichters schon etwas zu alt. Elizabeth
wiederum sah als zerbrechliche, sterbende Flora ein
wenig zu gesund aus. / Burton, en costume de samouraï,
craint d'être un peu trop vieux pour son rôle de poète,
tandis qu'Elizabeth est trop en forme pour incarner la
frêle et moribonde Flora.

"I believe in mind over matter and doing anything
you set your mind on."
Elizabeth Taylor

„Ich glaube an die Überlegenheit des Geistes
über die Materie, und dass man alles tun sollte,
was man sich in den Kopf gesetzt hat."
Elizabeth Taylor

« Je crois à la suprématie de l'esprit sur la matière
et à la nécessité de faire tout ce qui nous passe
par l'esprit. »
Elizabeth Taylor

STILL FROM 'BOOM' (1968)
The lady receives the angel of death, personified by
Burton. The film opened to negative reviews because
many critics aimed their barbs at the now notorious
couple rather than dealing with the merits of the film. /
Die Dame erhält Besuch vom Engel des Todes in der
Gestalt Burtons. Der Film wurde anfänglich verrissen,
weil viele Kritiker ihrem Unmut über das inzwischen
berüchtigte Ehepaar Luft machten, statt das Werk
objektiv zu beurteilen. / L'héroïne reçoit l'ange de la
mort, incarné par Burton. À sa sortie, le film reçoit les
traits acérés que la critique, sans se soucier de sa
qualité, décoche au couple désormais maudit.

STILL FROM 'SECRET CEREMONY' (1968)
Cenci (Mia Farrow) kidnaps prostitute Leonora
(Elizabeth), whom she believes to be her mother. /
Cenci (Mia Farrow) entführt die Prostituierte Leonora
(Elizabeth Taylor), die sie für ihre Mutter hält. / Cenci
(Mia Farrow) kidnappe la prostituée Leonora (Liz
Taylor), qu'elle croit être sa mère.

"One problem with people who have no vices is
that they're pretty sure to have some annoying
virtues."
Elizabeth Taylor

„Ein Problem mit Menschen, die keine Laster
haben, ist, dass sie mit ziemlicher Sicherheit
einige nervige Tugenden besitzen."
Elizabeth Taylor

« Le problème avec les gens qui n'ont pas de
vices, c'est qu'ils ont généralement des vertus
assez agaçantes. »
Elizabeth Taylor

STILL FROM 'SECRET CEREMONY' (1968)
They form a symbiotic relationship that verges on the
incestuous. / Die beiden bauen eine symbiotische
Beziehung auf, die an Inzest grenzt. / Les deux femmes
nouent une relation symbiotique et légèrement
incestueuse.

ON THE SET OF 'SECRET CEREMONY' (1968)
Losey (center) directs the couple in this psychological
thriller, which was again brutalized by critics. / Losey
(Mitte) führt bei diesem Pyschothriller Regie, der
ebenfalls von der Kritik völlig verrissen wurde. / Losey
(au centre) dirige les deux actrices dans ce thriller
psychologique à nouveau éreinté par la critique.

STILL FROM 'SECRET CEREMONY' (1968)
Cenci takes on the image of her mother as a form of
identification. / Cenci nimmt das Gesicht ihrer Mutter
als eine Form der Identifizierung an. / Cenci revêt
l'image de sa mère par désir d'identification.

ON THE SET OF 'ANNE OF THE THOUSAND DAYS' (1969)
Elizabeth grew up on the soundstages of Hollywood, so being on set with her husband felt like home to her. / Elizabeth wuchs in den Studios von Hollywood auf, sodass sie sich bei Dreharbeiten mit ihrem Ehemann wie zu Hause fühlte. / Ayant grandi dans les studios d'Hollywood, Elizabeth se sent chez elle sur un plateau en compagnie de son mari.

ON THE SET OF 'ANNE OF THE THOUSAND DAYS' (1969)
She appeared uncredited in the film. / Auch in diesem Film wird ihr Name nicht im Vor- oder Abspann genannt. / Elle apparaît incognito dans le film.

**ON THE SET OF 'THE ONLY GAME IN TOWN'
(1970)**
Even though the film is set in Las Vegas, the interiors
were filmed in Paris because contractually Elizabeth
and Richard could only be one hour apart from each
other. Here Elizabeth comforts aging director George
Stevens. / Obwohl der Film in Las Vegas spielt, wurden
die Innenaufnahmen in Paris gedreht, weil Elizabeth und
Richard laut Vertrag nicht mehr als eine Stunde von-
einander entfernt eingesetzt werden durften. Hier
erhält der alternde Regisseur George Stevens wieder
einmal ein paar Streicheleinheiten von Elizabeth. / Bien
que l'intrigue se déroule à Las Vegas, les intérieurs sont
filmés à Paris, car leurs contrats stipulent qu'Elizabeth
et Richard ne doivent jamais se trouver à plus d'une
heure de distance. L'actrice réconforte ici le réalisateur
vieillissant, George Stevens.

**STILL FROM 'THE ONLY GAME IN TOWN'
(1970)**
Taylor was originally slated to play opposite Frank
Sinatra. When the production was delayed, Warren
Beatty stepped in. / Taylor sollte ursprünglich an der
Seite von Frank Sinatra spielen. Als sich die Dreh-
arbeiten verzögerten, sprang Warren Beatty ein. / Le
partenaire de Liz Taylor devait être Frank Sinatra, mais
suite à des retards de tournage, il est remplacé par
Warren Beatty.

**STILL FROM 'THE ONLY GAME IN TOWN'
(1970)**
The chemistry between the two is obvious in their
scenes together. / Die „Chemie" zwischen den beiden
ist in ihren gemeinsamen Szenen offensichtlich. / Une
alchimie manifeste se produit entre les deux acteurs.

**ON THE SET OF 'THE ONLY GAME IN TOWN'
(1970)**
Burton, fearing the loss of his wife to Beatty, visited
the set often, much like Elizabeth visited his sets. /
Burton, der fürchtete, Beatty könne ihm seine Frau
ausspannen, besuchte sie oft bei den Dreharbeiten, so
wie Elizabeth ihn besuchte. / Craignant la concurrence
de Warren Beatty, Burton rend fréquemment visite à sa
femme, qui en fait autant.

STILL FROM 'X, Y AND ZEE' (1972)
Zee (Elizabeth Taylor) seeks revenge on her straying
husband (Michael Caine) by seducing his mistress. /
Zee (Elizabeth Taylor) will sich an ihrem untreuen
Ehemann (Michael Caine) rächen, indem sie seine
Geliebte verführt. / Zee (Elizabeth Taylor) tente de se
venger de son mari volage (Michael Caine) en séduisant
sa maîtresse.

"I don't pretend to be an ordinary housewife."
Elizabeth Taylor

„Ich gebe nicht vor, eine normale Hausfrau zu sein."
Elizabeth Taylor

*« Je ne prétends pas être une mère de famille
ordinaire. »*
Elizabeth Taylor

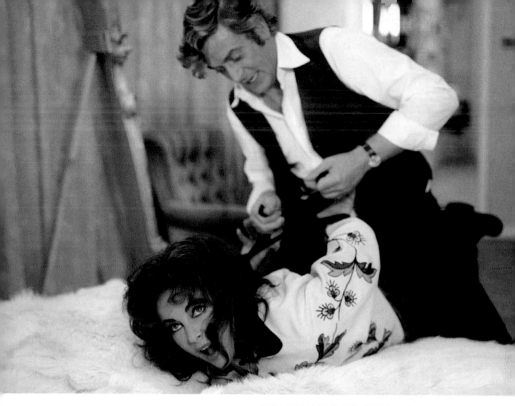

STILL FROM 'X, Y AND ZEE' (1972)
Michael Caine: "When you work with her, the people around her make it seem as if you're working with the Statue of Liberty!" / Michael Caine: „Wenn du mit ihr arbeitest, dann gibt dir ihr Hofstaat das Gefühl, du hättest es mit der Freiheitsstatue zu tun!" / Michael Caine : « Quand on travaille avec elle, les gens qui l'entourent font comme si vous tourniez avec la statue de la Liberté ! »

ON THE SET OF 'VILLAIN' (1971)
Elizabeth, unable to stay away from her amour fou,
visits the set of Burton's crime film. / Elizabeth, die sich
nicht von ihrem *amour fou* lösen kann, besucht Burton
bei den Dreharbeiten zu diesem Kriminalfilm. /
Incapable de rester éloignée de son grand amour,
Elizabeth se rend sur le tournage du film policier dans
lequel joue Burton.

*"I had a hollow leg. I could drink everyone under
the table and not get drunk. My capacity was
terrifying."*
Elizabeth Taylor

*„Ich hatte ein hohles Bein. Ich konnte jeden unter
den Tisch saufen, ohne betrunken zu werden.
Mein Trinkvermögen war erschreckend.“*
Elizabeth Taylor

*« J'avais une sacrée descente. Tout le monde
pouvait se retrouver sous la table et moi, je
n'étais toujours pas saoule. C'était terrifiant. »*
Elizabeth Taylor

STILL FROM 'UNDER MILK WOOD' (1972)
Captain Cat (Peter O'Toole, right) wanders the streets
of Llareggub recalling his sea adventures and whore
Rosie Probert (Elizabeth Taylor). Richard Burton
narrates the poetry of his beloved Welsh writer Dylan
Thomas. / Captain Cat (Peter O'Toole, rechts) irrt durch
die Straßen von Llareggub und erinnert sich an seine
Abenteuer zur See und mit der Hure Rosie Probert
(Elizabeth Taylor). Richard Burton spricht die Verse
seines geliebten walisischen Dichters Dylan Thomas. /
Captain Cat (Peter O'Toole) erre dans les rues de
Llareggub en se remémorant ses aventures en mer et sa
rencontre avec la putain Rosie Probert (Elizabeth
Taylor). Le narrateur est Richard Burton, grand
admirateur du poète gallois Dylan Thomas.

"**The beast is out of its cage,
these will be bloody times.**"

"**Hammersmith
Is Out**"ₓ

a **J. CORNELIUS CREAN FILMS, INC.** presentation

starring
ELIZABETH TAYLOR · RICHARD BURTON
PETER USTINOV · BEAU BRIDGES

Co-starring
Leon Ames · **Leon Askin** · **Anthony Holland** · **George Raft** · **John Schuck**

Directed by **PETER USTINOV** · Produced by **ALEX LUCAS** · Written by **STANFORD WHITMORE** · Music by **DOMINIC FRONTIERE** · Costumes by **EDITH HEAD**

IN COLOUR

NOW SHOWING AT ODEON ST. MARTIN'S LANE

STILL FROM 'HAMMERSMITH IS OUT' (1972)
The film was a disaster. The couple's relationship was dissolving and it showed on screen. Richard Burton: "Our natures do not inspire domestic tranquility." / Der Film war eine Katastrophe. Die Beziehung des Ehepaars war im Endstadium angekommen, und man konnte es auf der Leinwand sehen. Richard Burton: „Häuslicher Friede liegt uns nicht im Blut." / Ce film est un désastre, car la désagrégation du couple est visible à l'écran. Comme le dit Richard Burton, « nos tempéraments n'inspirent pas la tranquillité domestique ».

ADVERT FOR 'HAMMERSMITH IS OUT' (1972)
The film was marketed as a crime thriller in the style of 'Villain,' but it was a modern updating of 'Faust.' / Vermarktet wurde der Film als Kriminalthriller im Stil von *Die alles zur Sau machen*, aber in Wahrheit handelte es sich um einen moderne Version des *Faust*-Stoffes. / Vendu comme un thriller policier dans le style de *Salaud*, ce film est en réalité une transposition moderne de *Faust*.

**STILL FROM 'DIVORCE HIS/DIVORCE HERS'
(1973, TV)**
This TV movie showed the marriage break-up from
both points of view. Yet again, life and art intersect for
the couple. / Dieser Fernsehfilm zeigte den Zerfall
einer Ehe aus zwei Perspektiven. Wieder einmal
überschnitten sich für das Paar Kunst und Leben. /
Avec ce téléfilm qui présente le divorce selon le point
de vue des deux époux, la vie et l'art se reflètent à
nouveau pour les Burton.

STILL FROM 'NIGHT WATCH' (1973)
Ellen Wheeler (Elizabeth Taylor) is a woman on the
verge of a nervous breakdown. / Ellen Wheeler
(Elizabeth Taylor) ist eine Frau am Rande des
Nervenzusammenbruchs. / Ellen Wheeler (Elizabeth
Taylor), une femme au bord de la crise de nerfs.

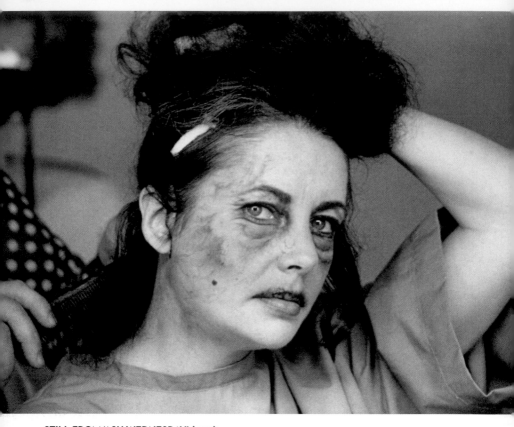

STILL FROM 'ASH WEDNESDAY' (1973)
Elizabeth takes on a subject which had not yet become
a cliché among Hollywood stars — plastic surgery. /
Elizabeth nimmt sich eines Themas an, das damals noch
nicht zum Klischee unter den Hollywood-Stars
geworden war: Schönheitschirurgie. / Ce film aborde un
sujet qui n'est pas encore devenu un cliché parmi les
stars d'Hollywood : la chirurgie esthétique.

"When you're fat, the world is divided into two
groups — people who bug you and people who
leave you alone. The funny thing is, supporters
and saboteurs exist in either camp."
Elizabeth Taylor

„Wenn du fett bist, dann teilt sich die Welt in zwei
Gruppen: Leute, die dich nerven, und Leute, die
dich in Ruhe lassen. Das Lustige ist, dass es in
beiden Lagern Befürworter und Saboteure gibt."
Elizabeth Taylor

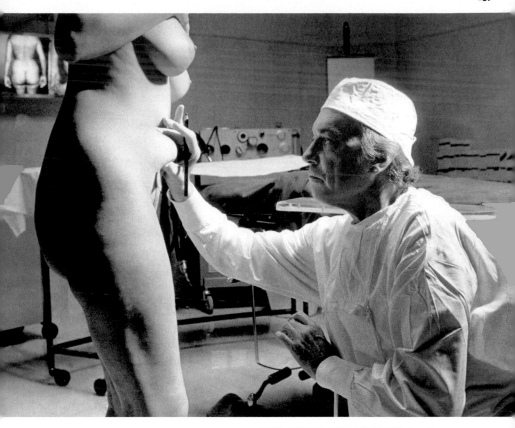

STILL FROM 'ASH WEDNESDAY' (1973)
Like the character in the movie, Elizabeth was not
immune to the search for eternal youth and sex
appeal. / Wie die Filmfigur war auch Elizabeth nicht
gegen die Sehnsucht nach ewiger Jugend und ewigem
Sex-Appeal gefeit. / Comme le personnage qu'elle
incarne, Elizabeth n'est pas insensible à la quête de la
jeunesse et de la séduction éternelles.

*« Quand on est gros, le monde se divise en deux
catégories : les gens qui vous embêtent et ceux qui
vous fichent la paix. Le plus drôle, c'est qu'il y a des
supporters et des saboteurs dans les deux camps. »*
Elizabeth Taylor

STILL FROM 'ASH WEDNESDAY' (1973)
She also had the opportunity to play against another Hollywood legend, Henry Fonda. / Der Film gab ihr auch die Gelegenheit, neben einer weiteren Hollywood-Legende zu spielen: Henry Fonda. / L'occasion de se confronter à une autre légende hollywoodienne, Henry Fonda.

STILL FROM 'ASH WEDNESDAY' (1973)
Elizabeth was still able to command $1 million per picture, plus gross points, because even her bad pictures made money. / Elizabeth konnte noch immer eine Million Dollar plus Gewinnbeteiligung für jeden Film verlangen, weil sogar ihre schlechten Filme Gewinn einspielten. / La star touche encore un cachet d'un million de dollars ainsi qu'un pourcentage sur les recettes, car même ses mauvais films rapportent.

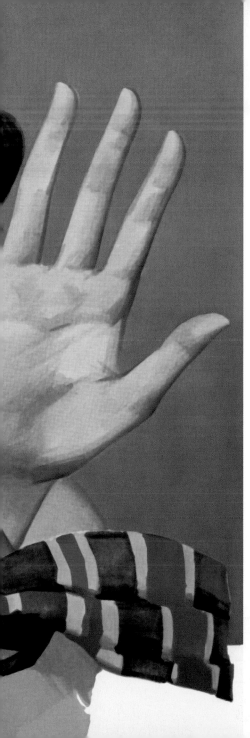

"I've been through it all, baby, I'm Mother Courage."
Elizabeth Taylor

„Ich hab alles schon durchgemacht, Baby. Ich bin Mutter Courage."
Elizabeth Taylor

« Rien ne m'a été épargné, chéri, je suis Mère Courage. »
Elizabeth Taylor

POSTER FOR 'IDENTIKIT' (1974)
This rarely seen film, also known as 'The Driver's Seat,' is about a woman searching all over Rome for a mystery lover. Much of it was improvised. / Dieser selten gezeigte Film, der auch unter dem Titel *The Driver's Seat* lief, handelt von einer Frau, die ganz Rom nach einem geheimnisvollen Liebhaber absucht. Ein Großteil des Films ist improvisiert. / Également appelé *The Driver's Seat*, ce film peu connu et en grande partie improvisé raconte l'histoire d'une femme sillonnant Rome à la recherche d'un mystérieux amant.

STILL FROM 'THE BLUE BIRD' (1976)
A rare attempt to achieve détente through art,
the musical adaptation of Maeterlinck's play was an
American-Russian co-production directed by 76-year-
old George Cukor. / Ein seltener Versuch, Ent-
spannungspolitik durch Kunst zu betreiben: Diese
musikalische Adaption des Theaterstücks *L'Oiseau bleu*
von Maurice Maeterlinck war eine amerikanisch-
russische Koproduktion unter der Regie des 76jährigen
George Cukor. / Rare tentative de réchauffement des
relations est-ouest à travers l'art, cette coproduction
américano-russe est une adaptation musicale de la
pièce éponyme de Maeterlinck (*L'Oiseau bleu*), réalisée
par George Cukor à l'âge de 76 ans.

STILL FROM 'THE BLUE BIRD' (1976)
Elizabeth played four parts in the film — Mother,
Witch (right), Queen of Light, and Maternal Love —
demonstrating once again that she had not lost her
range. / Elizabeth spielte in dem Film vier verschiedene
Rollen: Mutter, Hexe (rechts), Königin des Lichts und
Mutterliebe — und bewies wieder einmal, dass sie nichts
von ihrer Vielseitigkeit eingebüßt hatte. / Prouvant
qu'elle n'a rien perdu de sa polyvalence, Elizabeth
interprète quatre rôles dans le film : la mère, la sorcière
(ci-dessus), la lumière et l'amour maternel.

STILL FROM 'THE BLUE BIRD' (1976)
Two divas supreme of the American cinema, Elizabeth
and Ava Gardner. True to form, Elizabeth arrived at the
Leningrad Hotel with 2,800 pounds of luggage and an
entourage. / Zwei unübertreffliche Diven des
amerikanischen Kinos: Elizabeth Taylor und Ava
Gardner. Ihrem Ruf getreu erschien Elizabeth in ihrem
Leningrader Hotel mit 1.270 Kilogramm Gepäck und
einem großen Gefolge. / Deux divas du cinéma
américain, Liz Taylor et Ava Gardner. Fidèle à elle-
même, Elizabeth débarque à l'hôtel Leningrad avec sa
suite et plus d'une tonne de bagages.

STILL FROM 'THE BLUE BIRD' (1976)
The film followed two spoiled children who search
for the blue bird of happiness. / Der Film folgt zwei
verwöhnten Gören auf ihrer Suche nach dem blauen
Vogel der Glückseligkeit. / Ce film raconte l'histoire de
deux enfants gâtés en quête de l'oiseau du bonheur.

STILL FROM 'A LITTLE NIGHT MUSIC' (1978)
After her marriage to politician and future senator
John Warner, Elizabeth was radiant as the imperious
Desiree. / Nachdem sie den Politiker und späteren
Senator John Warner geheiratet hatte, glänzte
Elizabeth in der Rolle der anmaßenden Desirée. / Après
son mariage avec le politicien et futur sénateur John
Warner, Elizabeth se montre rayonnante dans le rôle de
la présomptueuse Désirée.

*"At least once a year I play a has-been actress ...
I'm a great success at playing has-beens."*
Elizabeth Taylor

*„Wenigstens einmal im Jahr spiele ich eine
Schauspielerin, die weg vom Fenster ist ... Ich bin
sehr erfolgreich darin, die Abgetakelte zu spielen."*
Elizabeth Taylor

*« Au moins une fois par an, je joue une actrice sur
le retour ... J'ai beaucoup de succès dans les rôles
de has-been. »*
Elizabeth Taylor

STILL FROM 'A LITTLE NIGHT MUSIC' (1978)
The brilliant Stephen Sondheim musical, based on
Ingmar Bergman's film 'Smiles of a Summer Night'
(1955), was shot on location in Vienna. Elizabeth's singing
voice was dubbed. / Das geistreiche Musical von
Stephen Sondheim nach dem Film *Das Lächeln einer
Sommernacht* (1955) von Ingmar Bergman wurde vor
Ort in Wien gedreht. Elizabeths Singstimme war
synchronisiert. / Cette brillante comédie musicale de
Stephen Sondheim, inspirée du film d'Ingmar Bergman
Sourires d'une nuit d'été (1955), est tournée sur place à
Vienne. Pour les parties chantées, la voix d'Elizabeth est
doublée.

STILL FROM 'THE MIRROR CRACK'D' (1980)
Now active in the world of politics, Elizabeth takes a
break to make an Agatha Christie mystery with her
friend Rock Hudson. / Elizabeth unterbricht ihre
politischen Aktivitäten, um mit ihrem Freund Rock
Hudson eine Krimiverfilmung nach Agatha Christie zu
drehen. / Activement engagée en politique, Elizabeth
se libère le temps de tourner avec son ami Rock
Hudson un film tiré d'un roman d'Agatha Christie.

"Acting is, to me now, artificial. Seeing people
suffer is real. It couldn't be more real. Some people
don't like to look at it in the face because it's
painful. But if nobody does, then nothing gets
done."
Elizabeth Taylor

„Die Schauspielerei ist für mich, zum
gegenwärtigen Zeitpunkt, etwas Künstliches.
Menschen leiden zu sehen, ist real. Es könnte gar
nicht realer sein. Manche Menschen schauen dem
nicht gern ins Gesicht, weil es schmerzt. Aber wenn
es niemand tut, dann geschieht auch nichts."
Elizabeth Taylor

STILL FROM 'THE MIRROR CRACK'D' (1980)
She takes the role of the fading actress, a role first
offered to Natalie Wood. / Sie spielt eine
Schauspielerin, deren Ruhm allmählich verblasst. Die
Rolle halte man zunächst Natalie Wood angeboten. /
Elle y incarne une actrice sur le retour, rôle d'abord
proposé à Natalie Wood.

« Aujourd'hui, le métier d'acteur me paraît artificiel.
Voir la souffrance d'autrui, voilà qui est réel. On ne
peut pas faire plus réel. Certains n'aiment pas la
regarder en face, car c'est pénible. Mais si
personne ne la regarde, on ne fait rien. »
Elizabeth Taylor

STILL FROM 'BETWEEN FRIENDS' (1983, TV)
In a TV movie, comedienne Carol Burnett meets
her idol, Elizabeth Taylor. Their comic rapport is
memorable. / In diesem Fernsehfilm trifft Komikerin
Carol Burnett ihr Idol Elizabeth Taylor. Die Überein-
stimmung zwischen den beiden ist erinnerungswert. /
Téléfilm marquant la rencontre de la comédienne Carol
Burnett avec son idole Elizabeth Taylor, dans un duo
comique mémorable.

**PORTRAIT FOR 'THE MIRROR CRACK'D'
(1980)**
As soon as the film wrapped she ran back to Detroit
to participate in the Republican convention with her
husband. / Sobald der Film abgedreht war, eilte sie nach
Detroit, um mit ihrem Mann am Parteitag der
Republikaner teilzunehmen. / Dès le tournage terminé,
elle se précipite à Detroit pour participer à la
convention républicaine avec son mari.

STILL FROM 'MALICE IN WONDERLAND' (1985, TV)

In what must have been a surreal experience, Elizabeth plays Louella Parsons, one of the two gossip columnists who hounded her throughout her early career. Jane Alexander portrayed the other infamous gadfly, Hedda Hopper. / Vermutlich war es eine surreale Erfahrung für Elizabeth, Louella Parsons zu spielen, eine der beiden Klatschkolumnistinnen, die ihr zu Beginn ihrer Karriere pausenlos auf den Fersen waren. Jane Alexander spielte die andere Nervensäge, Hedda Hopper. / Expérience un brin surréaliste, Elizabeth interprète Louella Parsons, l'une des deux journalistes « people » qui l'ont traquée au début de sa carrière. Jane Alexander incarne Hedda Hopper, sa redoutable consœur.

STILL FROM 'HOTEL' (1984, TV)

Elizabeth continues to venture into the world of commercial television, this time in a series. / Elizabeth machte weiterhin Abstecher in die Welt des kommerziellen Fernsehens, diesmal in einer Serie. / Elizabeth poursuit ses apparitions sur le petit écran, cette fois dans une série télévisée.

STILL FROM 'POKER ALICE' (1987, TV)
Elizabeth entered the Old West as the sassy "Poker"
Alice opposite Tom Skerritt. / Als kecke „Poker-Alice"
spielte Elizabeth an der Seite von Tom Skerritt in
diesem Fernsehwestern. / Liz Taylor au Far West en
impertinente joueuse de poker, avec Tom Skerritt pour
partenaire.

**PORTRAIT FOR 'THERE MUST BE A PONY'
(1986, TV)**
Another role as a fading actress, but this photo, with
co-star Robert Wagner, shows very little fading.
Elizabeth is as sensual and radiant as ever. / Eine
weitere Rolle als Schauspielerin, deren Ruhm verblasst.
Auf diesem Foto mit ihrem Kollegen Robert Wagner ist
allerdings von Verblassen keine Spur: Elizabeth sieht so
sinnlich und strahlend wie eh und je aus. / Bien qu'elle
interprète ici un rôle d'actrice sur le retour, Elizabeth
apparaît plus sensuelle et plus rayonnante que jamais
sur cette photo avec son partenaire Robert Wagner.

PAGE 178
PORTRAIT FOR 'THE V.I.P.s' (1963)
Elizabeth Taylor and Richard Burton. / Elizabeth Taylor
und Richard Burton. / Aux côtés de Richard Burton.

3
CHRONOLOGY

CHRONOLOGIE

CHRONOLOGIE

CHRONOLOGY

27 February 1932 Born in London.

1939 Fearing the coming war, parents move the family to California.

1942 Makes first film, *There's One Born Every Minute*; signs with MGM to make *Lassie Come Home*; loaned out to Fox for *Jane Eyre*.

1944 *National Velvet* catapults Taylor to child-star status.

1946 Writes a children's book called *Nibbles and Me*; parents separate.

1947 Both *Cynthia* and *Life with Father* establish Taylor as teenage star.

1949 *Little Women* released; appears on cover of *Time*.

1950 *Father of the Bride* opens. Marries hotelier Nicholas Hilton and divorces him within a year.

1951 Hospitalized due to a nervous breakdown. *A Place in the Sun* premieres to rave reviews and eventual awards.

1952 Marries actor Michael Wilding.

1953 Gives birth to son.

1955 Gives birth to second son.

1957 Divorces Wilding and marries Mike Todd. Gives birth to a girl.

1958 Todd killed in an airplane crash. *Cat on a Hot Tin Roof* opens.

1959 Marries singer Eddie Fisher. *Suddenly, Last Summer* opens.

1960 *BUtterfield 8* opens.

1961 Begins work on epic *Cleopatra*. Starts affair with costar Richard Burton. Hospitalized and almost dies. Wins an Academy Award for *BUtterfield 8*.

1963 *Cleopatra* opens to mediocre reviews but earns her $7m.

1964 Burton and Taylor marry. Taylor's autobiography published.

1966 The Taylor-Burton film *Who's Afraid of Virginia Woolf?* opens to rave reviews and earns Taylor another Academy Award.

1974 Burtons divorce.

1975 Burtons reconcile and remarry.

1976 Burtons divorce again.

1977–1978 Campaigns with new husband John Warner for the senate seat from Virginia. He wins, aided greatly by the hard work and fame of his wife.

1981 Stars on Broadway in *The Little Foxes*. Divorces John Warner.

1983 Burton and Taylor reunite on Broadway in Noel Coward's *Private Lives*. Checks into Betty Ford Clinic for treatment of addictions.

1984 Burton dies in Switzerland. Taylor begins working in television movies and episodic TV.

1986 Appears before congressional committee to plea for more AIDS research funding, beginning her two-decade campaign for AIDS awareness.

1987 Receives Légion d'honneur from France. Launches her perfumes.

1988 Meets fellow patient Larry Fortensky at Betty Ford Clinic. Her memoir/diet book *Elizabeth Takes Off* is published.

1991 Marries Fortensky.

1993 Receives Life Achievement Award from the American Film Institute.

1996 Divorces Fortensky.

1999 Named Dame of the British Empire by Queen Elizabeth II.

COVER OF 'THE LIFE AND LOVES OF LIZ TAYLOR' (1952)

The Life and Loves of

Liz Taylor

DELL

25c

"I have the
    body of a woman...
the emotions
        of a child..."
(see page 76)

CHRONOLOGIE

27. Februar 1932 Sie wird in London geboren.

1939 Aus Furcht vor dem bevorstehenden Krieg zieht die Familie nach Kalifornien.

1942 Sie dreht ihren ersten Film, *There's One Born Every Minute*, schließt einen Vertrag bei MGM ab, dreht *Heimweh* und wird für *Die Waise von Lowood* an Fox ausgeliehen.

1944 *Kleines Mädchen, großes Herz* macht Taylor schlagartig zum Kinderstar.

1946 Sie schreibt ein Kinderbuch mit dem Titel *Nibbles and Me*. Ihre Eltern trennen sich.

1947 Sowohl *Cynthia* als auch *Unser Leben mit Vater* etablieren Taylor als Teenagerstar.

1949 *Kleine tapfere Jo* kommt ins Kino; sie erscheint auf der Titelseite der Zeitschrift *Time*.

1950 *Der Vater der Braut* läuft an. Sie heiratet den Hotelier Nicholas Hilton und lässt sich nach weniger als einem Ehejahr wieder von ihm scheiden.

1951 Sie wird mit einem Nervenzusammenbruch ins Krankenhaus eingeliefert. *Ein Platz an der Sonne* wird bei der Uraufführung von der Kritik gepriesen und schließlich mit Preisen überhäuft.

1952 Sie heiratet den Schauspieler Michael Wilding.

1953 Sie bringt einen Sohn zur Welt.

1955 Sie bringt einen weiteren Sohn zur Welt.

1957 Sie lässt sich von Wilding scheiden und heiratet Mike Todd. Sie bringt ein Mädchen zur Welt.

1958 Todd kommt bei einem Flugzeugabsturz ums Leben. *Die Katze auf dem heißen Blechdach* läuft an.

1959 Sie heiratet den Sänger Eddie Fisher. *Plötzlich im letzten Sommer* läuft an.

1960 *Telefon Butterfield 8* läuft an.

1961 Sie beginnt mit der Arbeit an dem Filmepos *Cleopatra*. Sie fängt eine Affäre mit ihrem Kollegen

Richard Burton an. Sie wird ins Krankenhaus eingeliefert und stirbt fast. Sie wird für *Telefon Butterfield 8* mit einem Oscar ausgezeichnet.

1963 *Cleopatra* läuft an und bringt ihr trotz mittelmäßiger Kritiken 7 Millionen Dollar ein.

1964 Burton und Taylor heiraten. Taylors Autobiographie erscheint.

1966 Der Taylor/Burton-Film *Wer hat Angst vor Virginia Woolf?* wird von der Kritik gefeiert und beschert Taylor einen weiteren Oscar.

1974 Die Burtons lassen sich scheiden.

1975 Die Burtons heiraten wieder.

1976 Die Burtons lassen sich erneut scheiden.

1977–1978 Sie begleitet ihren neuen Ehemann John Warner im Wahlkampf für einen Sitz im Senat. Er gewinnt, nicht zuletzt dank der Unterstützung und harten Arbeit seiner berühmten Ehefrau.

1981 Sie spielt am Broadway eine Hauptrolle in *The Little Foxes*. Sie lässt sich von John Warner scheiden.

1983 Burton und Taylor stehen am Broadway wieder gemeinsam auf der Bühne in Noel Cowards *Private Lives*. Sie meldet sich wegen verschiedener Abhängigkeiten in der Betty-Ford-Klinik an.

1984 Burton stirbt in der Schweiz. Taylor beginnt, in Fernsehfilmen und -serien aufzutreten.

1986 Sie spricht vor einem Ausschuss des US-Kongresses und wirbt für eine größere finanzielle Unterstützung der AIDS-Forschung.

1987 Sie wird in die französische Ehrenlegion aufgenommen und bringt eine Parfümreihe heraus.

1988 Sie lernt in der Betty-Ford-Klinik den Mitpatienten Larry Fortensky kennen. Ihr mit Memoiren verknüpftes Diätbuch *Vom Dicksein, vom Dünnsein, vom Glücklichsein* erscheint.

1991 Sie heiratet Fortensky.

1993 Sie erhält vom American Film Institute den „Life Achievement Award" für ihr Lebenswerk.

1996 Sie lässt sich von Fortensky scheiden.

1999 Sie wird von Königin Elisabeth II. zur „Dame of the British Empire" ernannt.

CHRONOLOGIE

27 février 1932 Naissance à Londres.

1939 Par crainte de la guerre qui s'annonce, ses parents s'installent en Californie.

1942 Tourne son premier film, *There's One Born Every Minute*; signe avec la MGM pour *Fidèle Lassie*; est prêtée à la Fox pour *Jane Eyre*.

1944 *Le Grand National* la propulse au rang d'enfant star.

1946 Écrit un livre pour enfants intitulé *Nibbles and Me*; ses parents se séparent.

1947 *Cynthia* et *Mon père et nous* lui confèrent le statut de star adolescente.

1949 Sortie des *Quatre Filles du docteur March*; fait la couverture de *Time*.

1950 Sortie du *Père de la mariée*. Épouse le fondateur de la chaîne d'hôtels Hilton, Nick Hilton, dont elle divorce moins d'un an après.

1951 Hospitalisée pour dépression nerveuse. *Une place au soleil* obtient des critiques dithyrambiques et décrochera des prix.

1952 Épouse l'acteur Michael Wilding.

1953 Donne naissance à son premier fils.

1955 Donne naissance à son deuxième fils.

1957 Divorce de Wilding et épouse Mike Todd. Donne naissance à une fille.

1958 Todd meurt dans un accident d'avion. Sortie de *La Chatte sur un toit brûlant*.

1959 Épouse le chanteur Eddie Fisher. Sortie de *Soudain l'été dernier*.

1960 Sortie de *Vénus au vison*.

1961 Débute le tournage de *Cléopâtre*. Entame une liaison avec son partenaire Richard Burton. Est hospitalisée et frôle la mort. Remporte un oscar pour *Vénus au vison*.

1963 Malgré des critiques médiocres, *Cléopâtre* lui rapporte 7 millions de dollars.

1964 Épouse Richard Burton. Publie son autobiographie.

1966 Le couple Taylor-Burton reçoit des critiques élogieuses pour *Qui a peur de Virginia Woolf?*, qui vaut à l'actrice un nouvel oscar.

1974 Liz et Richard divorcent.

1975 Liz et Richard se réconcilient et se remarient.

1976 Liz et Richard divorcent à nouveau.

1977—1978 Épouse John Warner, dont elle soutient la campagne pour le siège de sénateur de Virginie; il le remporte en partie grâce à son dévouement et à sa célébrité.

1981 Joue à Broadway dans *The Little Foxes*. Divorce de John Warner.

1983 Retrouve Richard Burton à Broadway dans *Private Lives* de Noel Coward. Entre en cure de désintoxication à la clinique Betty Ford.

1984 Décès de Burton en Suisse. Tourne dans des téléfilms et des séries télévisées.

1986 Plaide devant une commission parlementaire pour l'octroi de fonds à la recherche contre le SIDA, s'engageant ainsi pour vingt ans dans la lutte contre cette maladie.

1987 Reçoit la Légion d'honneur en France. Lance une gamme de parfums.

1988 Rencontre Larry Fortensky à la clinique Betty Ford. Publie ses secrets de régime et de bien-être dans *Elizabeth dit tout*.

1991 Épouse Fortensky.

1993 L'American Film Institute lui décerne un prix pour l'ensemble de sa carrière.

1996 Divorce de Fortensky.

1999 Est anoblie par la reine Elizabeth II.

PORTRAIT (1993)

La **COLUMBIA PICTURES** presenta **LA PRODUZIONE DEI BURTON**

IL DOTTOR
FAUSTUS

4

FILMOGRAPHY

FILMOGRAFIE

FILMOGRAPHIE

There's One Born Every Minute (1942)
Gloria Twine. Director/Regie/réalisation: Harold Young.

Lassie Come Home (dt. *Heimweh*, fr. *Fidèle Lassie*, 1943)
Priscilla. Director/Regie/réalisation: Fred M. Wilcox.

Jane Eyre (dt. *Die Waise von Lowood*, 1944)
Helen Burns. Director/Regie/réalisation: Robert Stevenson.

The White Cliffs of Dover (dt. *Die weißen Klippen*, fr. *Les Blanches Falaises de Douvres*, 1944)
Betsy Kenney. Director/Regie/réalisation: Clarence Brown.

National Velvet (dt. *Kleines Mädchen, großes Herz*, fr. *Le Grand National*, 1944)
Velvet Brown. Director/Regie/réalisation: Clarence Brown.

Courage of Lassie (dt. *Lassie – Held auf vier Pfoten*, fr. *Le Courage de Lassie*, 1946)

Kathie Merrick. Director/Regie/réalisation: Fred M. Wilcox.

Life with Father (dt. *Unser Leben mit Vater*, fr. *Mon père et nous*, 1947)
Mary Skinner. Director/Regie/réalisation: Michael Curtiz.

Cynthia (1947)
Cynthia Bishop. Director/Regie/réalisation: Robert Z. Leonard.

A Date with Judy (dt. *Wirbel um Judy*, fr. *Ainsi sont les femmes*, 1948)
Carol Pringle. Director/Regie/réalisation: Richard Thorpe.

Julia Misbehaves (dt. *Julia benimmt sich schlecht*, fr. *La Belle Imprudente*, 1948)
Susan Packett. Director/Regie/réalisation: Jack Conway.

Little Women (dt. *Kleine tapfere Jo*, fr. *Les Quatre Filles du docteur March*, 1949)
Amy March. Director/Regie/réalisation: Mervyn LeRoy.

Conspirator (dt. *Verschwörer*, fr. *Guet-apens*, 1949)
Melinda Greyton. Director/Regie/réalisation: Victor Saville.

The Big Hangover (dt. *Von Katzen und Katern*, fr. *Le Chevalier de Bacchus*, 1950)
Mary Belney. Director/Regie/réalisation: Norman Krasna.

Father of the Bride (dt. *Der Vater der Braut*, fr. *Le Père de la mariée*, 1950)
Kay Banks. Director/Regie/réalisation: Vincente Minnelli.

Father's Little Dividend (dt. *Ein Geschenk des Himmels*, fr. *Allons donc, papa!*, 1951)
Kay Dunstan. Director/Regie/réalisation: Vincente Minnelli.

A Place in the Sun (dt. *Eine amerikanische Tragödie*, fr. *Une place au soleil*, 1951)
Angela Vickers. Director/Regie/réalisation: George Stevens.

Quo Vadis (1951)
Christian Prisoner/christliche Gefangene/prisonnière chrétienne. Director/Regie/réalisation: Mervyn LeRoy.

Love Is Better Than Ever (dt. *Die süße Falle*, fr. *Une vedette disparaît*, 1952)

Stacie Macaboy. Director/Regie/réalisation: Stanley Donen.

Ivanhoe (dt. *Ivanhoe – Der schwarze Ritter*, fr. *Ivanhoé*, 1952)
Rebecca. Director/Regie/réalisation: Richard Thorpe.

The Girl Who Had Everything (dt. *Ein verwöhntes Biest*, fr. *La Fille qui avait tout*, 1953)
Jean Latimer. Director/Regie/réalisation: Richard Thorpe.

Rhapsody (dt. *Symphonie des Herzens*, fr. *Rhapsodie*, 1954)
Louise Durant. Director/Regie/réalisation: Charles Vidor.

Elephant Walk (dt. *Elefantenpfad*, fr. *La Piste des éléphants*, 1954)
Ruth Wiley. Director/Regie/réalisation: William Dieterle.

Beau Brummell (dt. *Beau Brummell – Rebell und Verführer*, fr. *Le Beau Brummell*, 1954)
Lady Patricia Belham. Director/Regie/réalisation: Curtis Bernhardt.

The Last Time I Saw Paris (dt. *Damals in Paris*, fr. *La Dernière Fois que j'ai vu Paris*, 1954)
Helen Ellswirth. Director/Regie/réalisation: Richard Brooks.

Giant (dt. *Giganten*, fr. *Géant*, 1956)
Leslie Lynnton Benedict. Director/Regie/réalisation: George Stevens.

Raintree County (dt. *Das Land des Regenbaums*, fr. *L'Arbre de vie*, 1957)
Susanna Drake. Director/Regie/réalisation: Edward Dmytryk.

Cat on a Hot Tin Roof (dt. *Die Katze auf dem heißen Blechdach*, fr. *La Chatte sur un toit brûlant*, 1958)
Maggie Pollitt. Director/Regie/réalisation: Richard Brooks.

Suddenly, Last Summer (dt. *Plötzlich im letzten Sommer*, fr. *Soudain l'été dernier*, 1959)
Catherine Holly. Director/Regie/réalisation: Joseph L. Mankiewicz.

Scent of Mystery (1960)
"Real" Sally Kennedy/Die „echte" Sally Kennedy/La «vraie» Sally Kennedy. Director/Regie/réalisation: Jack Cardiff.

BUtterfield 8 (dt. *Telefon Butterfield 8*, fr. *Vénus au vison*, 1960)
Gloria Wandrous. Director/Regie/réalisation: Daniel Mann.

Cleopatra (fr. *Cléopâtre*, 1963)
Cleopatra/Cléopâtre. Director/Regie/réalisation: Joseph L. Mankiewicz.

The V.I.P.s (dt. *Hotel International*, fr. *Hôtel International*, 1963)
Frances Andros. Director/Regie/réalisation: Anthony Asquith.

The Sandpiper (dt. ... *die alles begehren*, fr. *Le Chevalier des sables*, 1965)
Laura Reynolds. Director/Regie/réalisation: Vincente Minnelli.

Who's Afraid of Virginia Woolf? (dt. *Wer hat Angst vor Virginia Woolf?*, fr. *Qui a peur de Virginia Woolf ?*, 1966)
Martha. Director/Regie/réalisation: Mike Nichols.

The Taming of the Shrew (dt. *Der Widerspenstigen Zähmung*, fr. *La Mégère apprivoisée*, 1967)
Katharina. Director/Regie/réalisation: Franco Zeffirelli.

Doctor Faustus (1967)
Helen of Troy/Helena von Troja/Hélène de Troie.
Directors/Regie/réalisation: Richard Burton, Nevill Coghill.

Reflections in a Golden Eye (dt. *Spiegelbild im goldenen Auge*, fr. *Reflet dans un œil d'or*, 1967)
Leonora Penderton. Director/Regie/réalisation: John Huston.

The Comedians (dt. *Die Stunde der Komödianten*, fr. *Les Comédiens*, 1967)
Martha Pineda. Director/Regie/réalisation: Peter Glenville.

Boom (dt. *Brandung*, 1968)
Flora Goforth. Director/Regie/réalisation: Joseph Losey.

Secret Ceremony (dt. *Die Frau aus dem Nichts*, fr. *Cérémonie secrète*, 1968)
Leonora. Director/Regie/réalisation: Joseph Losey.

Anne of the Thousand Days (dt. *Königin für tausend Tage*, fr. *Anne des mille jours*, 1969)
Courtesan/Kurtisane/Courtisane.
Director/Regie/réalisation: Charles Jarrott.

The Only Game in Town (dt. *Das einzige Spiel in der Stadt*, fr. *Las Vegas ... un couple*, 1970)
Fran Walker. Director/Regie/réalisation: George Stevens.

X, Y and Zee (dt. *X, Y und Zee*, fr. *Une belle tigresse*, 1972)
Zee Blakeley. Director/Regie/réalisation: Brian G. Hutton.

Under Milk Wood (1972)
Rosie Probert. Director/Regie/réalisation: Andrew Sinclair.

Hammersmith Is Out (dt. *Hammersmith ist raus*, fr. *Liberté provisoire*, 1972)
Jimmie Jean Jackson. Director/Regie/réalisation: Peter Ustinov.

Divorce His/Divorce Hers (dt. *Seine Scheidung – ihre Scheidung*, fr. *Divorce*, 1973, TV)
Jane Reynolds. Director/Regie/réalisation: Waris Hussein.

Night Watch (dt. *Die Nacht der tausend Augen*, fr. *Terreur dans la nuit*, 1973)
Ellen Wheeler. Director/Regie/réalisation: Brian G. Hutton.

Ash Wednesday (dt. *Die Rivalin*, fr. *Les Noces de cendre*, 1973)
Barbara Sawyer. Director/Regie/réalisation: Larry Peerce.

Identikit (1974)
Lise. Director/Regie/réalisation: Giuseppe Patroni Griffi.

The Blue Bird (dt. *Der blaue Vogel*, fr. *L'Oiseau bleu*, 1976)
Light/Mother/Witch/Maternal Love.
Licht/Mutter/Hexe/Mutterliebe.
La mère/la sorcière/la lumière/l'amour maternel.
Director/Regie/réalisation: George Cukor.

Victory at Entebbe (dt. *Unternehmen Entebbe*, fr. *Victoire à Entebbé*, 1976, TV)
Edra Vilnofsky. Director/Regie/réalisation: Marvin Chomsky.

A Little Night Music (dt. *Das Lächeln einer Sommernacht*, fr. *Petite musique de nuit*, 1978)
Desirée Armfeldt. Director/Regie/réalisation: Harold Prince.

Return Engagement (1978, TV)
Dr. Emily Loomis. Director/Regie/réalisation: Joseph Hardy.

METRO-GOLDWYN-MAYER PRESENTS
ELIZABETH TAYLOR
LAURENCE HARVEY
EDDIE FISHER

IN JOHN O'HARA'S
BUTTERFIELD 8

The most desirable woman in town – and the easiest to find....Just dial BUTterfield 8

Cert.X · in CinemaScope and Metrocolor co-starring DINA MERRILL

MILDRED DUNNOCK · BETTY FIELD · JEFFREY LYNN · KAY MEDFORD · SUSAN OLIVER · Screen Play by CHARLES SCHNEE and JOHN MICHAEL HAYES Directed by DANIEL MANN · A PANDRO S. BERMAN PRODUCTION

Winter Kills (dt. *Philadelphia Clan*, 1979)
Lola Comante. Director/Regie/réalisation: William Richert.

The Mirror Crack'd (dt. *Mord im Spiegel*, fr. *Le miroir se brisa*, 1980)
Marina Gregg. Director/Regie/réalisation: Guy Hamilton.

Between Friends (dt. *Freundinnen fürs Leben*, 1983, TV)
Deborah Shapiro. Director/Regie/réalisation: Lou Antonio.

Malice in Wonderland (dt. *Verrücktes Hollywood*, fr. *Traquées*, 1985, TV)
Louella Parsons. Director/Regie/réalisation: Gus Trikonis.

North and South (dt. *Fackeln im Sturm*, fr. *Nord et Sud*, 1985, TV)
Madam Conti. Director/Regie/réalisation: Richard T. Heffron.

There Must Be a Pony (dt. *Schatten des Ruhms*, fr. *Une vie de star*, 1986, TV)
Marguerite Sydney. Director/Regie/réalisation: Joseph Sargent.

Poker Alice (1987, TV)

Alice Moffett. Director/Regie/réalisation: Arthur A. Seidelman.

Giovane Toscanini (fr. *Toscanini*, 1988)
Nadina Bulichoff. Director/Regie/réalisation: Franco Zeffirelli.

Sweet Bird of Youth (dt. *Süßer Vogel Jugend*, fr. *Doux oiseau de jeunesse*, 1989, TV)
Alexandra Del Lago. Director/Regie/réalisation: Nicolas Roeg.

The Flintstones (dt. *Familie Feuerstein*, fr. *La Famille Pierrafeu*, 1994)
Pearl Slaghoople. Director/Regie/réalisation: Brian Levant.

Those Old Broads (dt. *Diese alten Biester*, 2001, TV)
Beryl Mason. Director/Regie/réalisation: Matthew Diamond.

Television series/Fernsehserien/Séries TV:

General Hospital (1981)

All My Children (1983, 1984)

Hotel (1984)

The Simpsons (1992)

God, the Devil and Bob (2000)

BIBLIOGRAPHY

Adler, Bill: *Elizabeth Taylor: Triumphs and Tragedies.* Ace, 1982.
Amblin, Ellis: *The Most Beautiful Woman in the World.* Harper Collins, 2000.
Bozzacchi, Gianni: *Elizabeth Taylor: The Queen and I.* University of Wisconsin Press, 2002.
Bragg, Melvyn: *Richard Burton.* Little, Brown, 1988.
Branin, Larissa: *Liz: The Pictorial Biography of Elizabeth Taylor.* Courage, 2000.
Brodsky, Jack & Weiss, Nathan: *The Cleopatra Papers.* Simon and Schuster, 1963.
Christopher, James & Christophe: *Elizabeth Taylor.* Deutsch, 1999.
David, Lester & Robbins, Jhan: *Richard and Elizabeth.* Funk and Wagnalls, 1977.
Heymann, C. David: *Liz: An Intimate Biography of Elizabeth Taylor.* Carol, 1995.
Hirsch, Foster: *Elizabeth Taylor.* Pyramid, 1973.
Kelley, Kitty: *Elizabeth Taylor: The Last Star.* Dell, 1981.
Maddox, Brenda with Fisher, David: *Been There, Done That.* St. Martin's, 1999.
Maddox, Brenda: *Who's Afraid of Elizabeth Taylor?.* M. Evans and Co., 1977.

Nickens, Chris: *Elizabeth Taylor.* Dolphin, 1994.
Robin-Tani, Marianne: *The New Elizabeth.* St. Martin's, 1988.
Sakol, Jeannie & Latham, Caroline: *All about Elizabeth Taylor: Public and Private.* Onyx, 1991.
Sheppard, Dick: *Elizabeth.* Warner, 1974.
Spoto, Donald: *A Passion for Life: The Biography of Elizabeth Taylor.* Harpercollins, 1996.
Taraborrelli, J. Randy: *Elizabeth.* Warner, 2006.
Taylor, Elizabeth: *Elizabeth Takes Off.* Putnam's, 1980.
Taylor, Elizabeth: *Elizabeth Taylor.* Harper and Row, 1964.
Taylor, Elizabeth: *My Love Affair with Jewelry.* Simon and Schuster, 2003.
Taylor, Elizabeth: *Nibbles and Me.* Duell, Sloan & Pearce, 1946.
Vermilye, Jerry & Ricci, Mark: *The Films of Elizabeth Taylor.* Carol, 1993.
Walker, Alexander: *Elizabeth.* Weidenfeld and Nicolson, 1990.
Waterbury, Ruth & Arceri, Gene: *Elizabeth Taylor: Her Life, Her Loves, Her Future.* Bantam, 1982.
Willoughby, Bob: *Liz, an Intimate Collection: Photographs of Elizabeth Taylor.* Merrell, 2004.

IMPRINT

© 2008 TASCHEN GmbH
Hohenzollernring 53, D–50672 Köln
www.taschen.com

Editor/Picture Research/Layout: Paul Duncan/Wordsmith Solutions
Editorial Coordination: Martin Holz and Katharina Krause, Cologne
Production Coordination: Nadia Najm and Horst Neuzner, Cologne
German Translation: Thomas J. Kinne, Nauheim
French Translation: Anne Le Bot, Paris
Multilingual Production: www.arnaudbriand.com, Paris
Typeface Design: Sense/Net, Andy Disl and Birgit Reber, Cologne

Printed in Italy
ISBN 978-3-8228-2322-4

To stay informed about upcoming TASCHEN titles, please request our magazine at www.taschen.com/magazine or write to TASCHEN, Hohenzollernring 53, D-50672 Cologne, Germany, contact@taschen.com, Fax: +49-221-254919. We will be happy to send you a free copy of our magazine which is filled with information about all of our books.

All the photos in this book were supplied by The Kobal Collection. Thanks to Dave Kent, Phil Moad and everybody at The Kobal Collection for their professionalism and kindness.

METRO·GOLDWYN·MAYER presents

ELIZABETH TAYLOR
LAURENCE HARVEY
EDDIE FISHER

IN JOHN O'HARA'S

BUTTERFIELD 8

The most desirable woman in town – and the easiest to find....Just dial BUTterfield 8

Cert 'X' · CinemaScope and Metrocolor co-starring DINA MERRILL

MILDRED DUNNOCK · BETTY FIELD · JEFFREY LYNN · KAY MEDFORD · SUSAN OLIVER · Screen Play by CHARLES SCHNEE and JOHN MICHAEL HAYES · Directed by DANIEL MANN · A PANDRO S. BERMAN PRODUCTION

Winter Kills (dt. *Philadelphia Clan*, 1979)
Lola Comante. Director/Regie/réalisation: William Richert.

The Mirror Crack'd (dt. *Mord im Spiegel*, fr. *Le miroir se brisa*, 1980)
Marina Gregg. Director/Regie/réalisation: Guy Hamilton.

Between Friends (dt. *Freundinnen fürs Leben*, 1983, TV)
Deborah Shapiro. Director/Regie/réalisation: Lou Antonio.

Malice in Wonderland (dt. *Verrücktes Hollywood*, fr. *Traquées*, 1985, TV)
Louella Parsons. Director/Regie/réalisation: Gus Trikonis.

North and South (dt. *Fackeln im Sturm*, fr. *Nord et Sud*, 1985, TV)
Madam Conti. Director/Regie/réalisation: Richard T. Heffron.

There Must Be a Pony (dt. *Schatten des Ruhms*, fr. *Une vie de star*, 1986, TV)
Marguerite Sydney. Director/Regie/réalisation: Joseph Sargent.

Poker Alice (1987, TV)

Alice Moffett. Director/Regie/réalisation: Arthur A. Seidelman.

Giovane Toscanini (fr. *Toscanini*, 1988)
Nadina Bulichoff. Director/Regie/réalisation: Franco Zeffirelli.

Sweet Bird of Youth (dt. *Süßer Vogel Jugend*, fr. *Doux oiseau de jeunesse*, 1989, TV)
Alexandra Del Lago. Director/Regie/réalisation: Nicolas Roeg.

The Flintstones (dt. *Familie Feuerstein*, fr. *La Famille Pierrafeu*, 1994)
Pearl Slaghoople. Director/Regie/réalisation: Brian Levant.

Those Old Broads (dt. *Diese alten Biester*, 2001, TV)
Beryl Mason. Director/Regie/réalisation: Matthew Diamond.

Television series/Fernsehserien/Séries TV:

General Hospital (1981)

All My Children (1983, 1984)

Hotel (1984)

The Simpsons (1992)

God, the Devil and Bob (2000)

BIBLIOGRAPHY

Adler, Bill: Elizabeth Taylor: Triumphs and Tragedies. Ace, 1982.

Amblin, Ellis: The Most Beautiful Woman in the World. Harper Collins, 2000.

Bozzacchi, Gianni: Elizabeth Taylor: The Queen and I. University of Wisconsin Press, 2002.

Bragg, Melvyn: Richard Burton. Little, Brown, 1988.

Branin, Larissa: Liz: The Pictorial Biography of Elizabeth Taylor. Courage, 2000.

Brodsky, Jack & Weiss, Nathan: The Cleopatra Papers. Simon and Schuster, 1963.

Christopher, James & Christophe: Elizabeth Taylor. Deutsch, 1999.

David, Lester & Robbins, Jhan: Richard and Elizabeth. Funk and Wagnalls, 1977.

Heymann, C. David: Liz: An Intimate Biography of Elizabeth Taylor. Carol, 1995.

Hirsch, Foster: Elizabeth Taylor. Pyramid, 1973.

Kelley, Kitty: Elizabeth Taylor: The Last Star. Dell, 1981.

Maddox, Brenda with Fisher, David: Been There, Done That. St. Martin's, 1999.

Maddox, Brenda: Who's Afraid of Elizabeth Taylor?. M. Evans and Co., 1977.

Nickens, Chris: Elizabeth Taylor. Dolphin, 1994.

Robin-Tani, Marianne: The New Elizabeth. St. Martin's, 1988.

Sakol, Jeannie & Latham, Caroline: All about Elizabeth Taylor: Public and Private. Onyx, 1991.

Sheppard, Dick: Elizabeth. Warner, 1974.

Spoto, Donald: A Passion for Life: The Biography of Elizabeth Taylor. Harpercollins, 1996.

Taraborrelli, J. Randy: Elizabeth. Warner, 2006.

Taylor, Elizabeth: Elizabeth Takes Off. Putnam's, 1980.

Taylor, Elizabeth: Elizabeth Taylor. Harper and Row, 1964.

Taylor, Elizabeth: My Love Affair with Jewelry. Simon and Schuster, 2003.

Taylor, Elizabeth: Nibbles and Me. Duell, Sloan & Pearce, 1946.

Vermilye, Jerry & Ricci, Mark: The Films of Elizabeth Taylor. Carol, 1993.

Walker, Alexander: Elizabeth. Weidenfeld and Nicolson, 1990.

Waterbury, Ruth & Arceri, Gene: Elizabeth Taylor: Her Life, Her Loves, Her Future. Bantam, 1982.

Willoughby, Bob: Liz, an Intimate Collection: Photographs of Elizabeth Taylor. Merrell, 2004.

IMPRINT

© 2008 TASCHEN GmbH
Hohenzollernring 53, D–50672 Köln
www.taschen.com

Editor/Picture Research/Layout: Paul Duncan/Wordsmith Solutions
Editorial Coordination: Martin Holz and Katharina Krause, Cologne
Production Coordination: Nadia Najm and Horst Neuzner, Cologne
German Translation: Thomas J. Kinne, Nauheim
French Translation: Anne Le Bot, Paris
Multilingual Production: www.arnaudbriand.com, Paris
Typeface Design: Sense/Net, Andy Disl and Birgit Reber, Cologne

Printed in Italy
ISBN 978-3-8228-2322-4

To stay informed about upcoming TASCHEN titles, please request our magazine at www.taschen.com/magazine or write to TASCHEN, Hohenzollernring 53, D-50672 Cologne, Germany, contact@taschen.com, Fax: +49-221-254919. We will be happy to send you a free copy of our magazine which is filled with information about all of our books.

All the photos in this book were supplied by The Kobal Collection. Thanks to Dave Kent, Phil Moad and everybody at The Kobal Collection for their professionalism and kindness.